The Medical Transcriptionist's Handbook

Rachelle S. Blake, B.A., R.M.T.
Chief Executive Officer
JurisMedico Transcription Service, Inc.
Founder
The Transcription Institute
Denver, Colorado

SOUTH-WESTERN PUBLISHING CO.

Library of Congress Cataloging-in-Publication Data

Blake, Rachelle S.
    The medical transcriptionist's handbook / Rachelle S. Blake.
        p.   cm.
    Includes bibliographical references and index.
    ISBN 0-538-70677-5
    1. Medical transcription--Handbooks, manuals, etc.   I. Title.
    [DNLM: 1. Medical Records--handbooks.   2. Medical Secretaries-
-handbooks.]
    R728.8B54   1993
    W 39 B636m
    653'.18--dc20
    DNLC/DLC
for Library of Congress   91-4687
                                                                         CIP

4 5 6 7 8 9 0 BB 98 97 96

Printed in the United States of America

Managing Editor: Betty R. Schechter
Developmental Editor: Inell Bolls-Gaither
Production Editor: Karen Roberts
Editorial Production Manager: Linda R. Allen
Production Artist: Sophia Renieris
Associate Photo Editor/Stylist: Linda Ellis

Preface

Direction and objective: *The Medical Transcriptionist's Handbook* is directed to students of medical transcription as well as currently practicing medical transcriptionists who work in hospitals, clinics, physician's offices and professional medical transcription services. The objective of this handbook is to provide medical transcriptionists with the following:

- a compilation of comprehensive answers to common questions and problems encountered when transcribing medical dictation

- a medical perspective to the documentation of records

- a source of basic information and guidelines for style, grammar and specific medical transcription mechanics

- a fundamental training manual including end-of-text exercises for the student of medical transcription

- a practical supplement to the medical transcriptionist's personal library of medical texts, word books, dictionaries and grammar books

Features: *The Medical Transcriptionist's Handbook* features a unit-by-unit breakdown of medical transcription mechanics such as abbreviations, numbers, plural and possessive forms, and capitalization. The handbook includes not only general guidelines, examples and applications for basic medical transcription, but it offers in-depth coverage of editing techniques, spelling techniques and techniques for formatting medical records as well. Key words are indicated in bold print for Units 1 through 5. The user of this text should be able to define these words upon completion of each unit. Additionally the key words may be used as study aids. The text also includes a number of appendices providing the medical transcriptionist with specialized information on word processing, common medical terms, medical symbols and reference values for common laboratory data.

Although other texts in medical transcription exist, *The Medical Transcriptionist's Handbook* is unique in that it serves as both a reference manual and a textbook. Potential transcriptionists can use the text in their studies and then go on to keep and continue to use the book in their daily work as medical transcriptionists.

Organization: Each unit in *The Medical Transcriptionist's Handbook* begins with an overview, or summary, of the unit's particular focus. Further, each unit contains detailed explanations and specific examples of the concepts being introduced. Additionally, end-of-text activities provide a study aid that will help the student of medical transcription absorb more fully the topics covered in each unit. Practice tests are also provided to insure proper preparation for in-class examinations.

Instructor's Supplements: The accompanying instructor's manual to *The Medical Transcriptionist's Handbook* includes an overview for each part presented in the handbook along with criterion performance objectives that the student should achieve for each unit. The manual also contains multiple-choice quizzes and supplementary objective tests consisting of multiple-choice, short answer, matching questions and test answers.

About the Author: Rachelle Blake, author of *The Medical Transcriptionist's Handbook*, has been involved in the legal and medical transcription industry for over 10 years. She has served in the capacities of medical office clerk, medical transcriptionist, medical office administrator, medical transcription supervisor, medical transcription service operations manager, instructor in medical transcription and chief executive officer of a major metropolitan medical and legal transcription service. She attended the University of Denver, with a dual major of mass communications and biology, has served several internships and apprenticeships, and has been trained and employed in hospitals, clinics and physicians' offices nationwide. She has taught at Denver Technical College and is founder of The Transcription Institute. She has served as chief executive officer of JurisMedico Transcription Service, Inc., for the past five years. She also currently supervises the contract medical transcription services for Humana Hospital Mountain View, Thornton, Colorado; Mercy Medical Center, Pathology Department, Denver, Colorado; and Aurora Associates of Otolaryngology, Aurora, Colorado.

Acknowledgments: I would like to thank the following persons for the inspiration, help, advice and support they have given me throughout my career as a medical transcriptionist, medical transcription service manager/owner, instructor and author. I also gratefully acknowledge all those who have aided in the creation of this book. Without these individuals, this project would not have been possible:

My family, including my husband, Richard Roy Blake, without whose love and support this work could not have been created; my beloved mother, Lettie Annette Scott; my father, John Scott, Sr.; Floyd and Connie Blake; Bessie Elizabeth Craddock; J. Richard Peck; John A. Scott, II; and Kai A. I. Scott. Those who inspired and assisted me in the development of this book, including: Susan Brodie; The Students of DTC Class MED 125—Summer '89, Fall '89 and Winter '90; Robin B. Anderson; H. Patrick Carr, M.D.; Jerry L. Cupps, D.O.; Linda Houlihan; Irene Hughes; Rick W. Rasband, M.D.; Diane Schauger; and Arlene Atchison Stolte.

Rachelle S. Blake

Contents

Practice Tests

Appendices

Bibliography

Index

Part One

Introduction to Medical Transcription

1

Unit 1

What Is Medical Transcription?

Overview: Welcome to the exciting and challenging career of medical transcription. The author hopes you will find this handbook helpful in performing your duties as a medical transcriptionist, and that this handbook will save a great deal of time for you in finding the proper word, format or method to use when transcribing. Before we dive into the great wealth of mechanics the medical transcriptionist uses, however, let us first ask ourselves: *What is medical transcription, and what do medical transcriptionists do?*

1-A   A Brief History of Medicine

Medicine, the preservation of health, the prevention of illness, and the treatment of disease processes, is one of the most basic elements of life. With its earliest foundations based in religion, medicine was first practiced thousands of years ago, in the Stone Age. Unfortunately, the Neanderthal man did not have a written alphabet, so he was unable to leave a record of his medical concepts and philosophy.

Later medicine was practiced by medicine men, or "shamans." To early Native Americans, medicine included anything having a religious or therapeutic orientation, from objects such as bows, arrowheads or stones, to injuries such as a lacerated arm, a bruised leg or a wounded knee. These men of medicine practiced or "made" medicine, either through the use of ceremony or natural herbs and preparations. Unfortunately, however, the techniques the medicine men used were still not easily passed on; documentation, in the form of petroglyphs or picture-writing on rocks, was crude and limited, and simple picture representations of treatments often were confused or misunderstood.

More advanced documentation of medicine was accomplished during the fourth and fifth centuries B.C. It is generally accepted that the art of practicing medicine as a documented scientific method was begun by the Greek physician Hippocrates in about 500 B.C. Hippocrates authored a collection of works known as the Hippocratic Corpus, which includes what is called the Hippocratic Oath, an oath physicians take upon their entrance into the field (Figure 1).

FIGURE 1   The Hippocratic Oath

HIPPOCRATIC OATH

"I swear by Apollo the physician, and Aesculapius, and Hygeia, and Panacea, and all the gods and goddesses, that according to my ability and judgment, I will keep this oath and its stipulation—to reckon him who taught me this art equally dear to me as my parents, to share my substance with him, and to relieve his necessities if required; to look upon his offspring in the same footing as my own brothers, and to teach them this art if they shall wish to learn it, without fee or stipulation, and that by precept, lecture, and every other mode of instruction, I will impart a knowledge of the art to my own sons, and those of my teachers, and to disciples bound by a stipulation and oath according to the law of medicine, but to none other.

"I will follow that system of regimen which, according to my ability and judgment, I consider for the benefit of my patients, and abstain from whatever is deleterious and mischievous. I will give no deadly medicine to anyone if asked, nor suggest any such counsel; and in like manner I will not give to a woman a pessary to produce abortion. With purity and with holiness I will pass my life and practice my art. I will not cut persons laboring under the stone, but will leave this to be done by men who are practitioners of this work. Into whatever houses I enter, I will go into them for the benefit of the sick, and I will abstain from every voluntary act of mischief and corruption; and, further, from the seduction of females or males, of freemen and slaves. Whatever, in connection with my professional practice, or not in connection with it, I see or hear, in the life of men, which ought not to be spoken of abroad, I will not divulge, as reckoning that all such should be kept secret.

"While I continue to keep this Oath unviolated, may it be granted to me to enjoy life and the practice of this art, respected by all men, in all times. But should I trespass and violate this Oath, may the reverse be my lot."

Courtesy of *Taber's Cyclopedic Medical Dictionary*. 16th ed. Edited by Clayton L. Thomas. (Philadelphia: F.A. Davis Co., 1989)

As you can see, the documentation and recording of medical procedure and theory is an essential link in the history of medicine. You, as a medical transcriptionist, continue the chain by documenting the art and practice of medicine.

1-B   The Medical Transcription Process

What Is Medical Transcription? Medical transcription is taking written or dictated medical information and producing a permanent, uniform record of that information, usually in typewritten or word-processed form. The medical information can vary from the records of a patient's visit to the physician, to a specific hospital report such as a pathology or a radiology report, to a manuscript for publication regarding medical or scientific topics. The information in almost all cases is confidential and should always be treated with sensitivity, privacy and respect. (See Hippocratic Oath, Figure 1.) Medical records have the potential to be subpoenaed in a court of law and therefore should be regarded as legal documentation. Medical transcription, once complete, should at all times be kept orderly, tidy and professional appearing.

Who Are Medical Transcriptionists? Medical transcriptionists are men or women who produce permanent and uniform medical records and information. Medical transcriptionists are an integral part of the allied health professional team—the nurses, office managers and staff, physician's and medical assistants, and others whose primary task is to work with the physician in providing medical care. Medical transcriptionists are part secretary, part translator, part editor, and part physician's assistant. They sometimes work in hospitals, sometimes work in medical offices or clinics, sometimes work for professional medical transcription services independent of hospitals or clinics, and sometimes work at home for themselves or subcontracting for a medical transcription service.

Medical transcriptionists many times need to work independently or with minimal supervision; therefore, discipline and self-commitment are important requirements for becoming a successful medical transcriptionist. Medical transcriptionists must develop skills in listening, mental deciphering, hand-eye coordination and concentration, and in working in a high-pressure environment where there is a specific time in which the transcription task must be completed. They must also be prepared to deal with a variety of regional dialects, accents, colloquialisms and foreign language variations.

All medical transcriptionists must be well-trained in a variety of disciplines: **grammar** (the study of words and their roles in a sentence), **keyboarding/word processing** (saving text in a computer's memory or on a magnetized diskette instead of on a piece of paper), and **medical terminology** (words specifically related to the medical field). Transcriptionists need to be able to make legible, logical and comprehensible reports out of oral or written documents that were previously lacking in one or all of these qualities.

Learning how to do medical transcription is not extremely difficult, yet it is challenging; therefore, constant consistent study, self-motivation and true dedication are all important requisites.

What Knowledge Is Necessary Regarding Words and How to Use Them?
Exhaustive knowledge of words and how to use them is necessary in becoming a successful medical transcriptionist. A transcriptionist must be fluent in different forms of word breakdowns, such as **phonemics** (keys to pronunciation), **etymology** (study of word origins), **phraseology** (the study of sentences and phrases), as well as the use of **acronyms** (words that are made from the first letter of a group of words), **homonyms** (words that are spelled alike and pronounced alike, but are different in meaning), **synonyms** (words with alike meanings), and **antonyms** (words with opposite meaning).

What Does A Medical Transcriptionist Have To Know About Editing?
Editing (assembling or reassembling a word, group of words or **document**—one or more pages of text—by cutting, pasting, adding, deleting and rearranging) is another important component to medical transcription. A medical transcriptionist has to know when, as well as how, to edit. Some of the tools she or he must use in editing include using correct words, grammar, punctuation, numbers, abbreviations, plurals, possessives, compound words, pronouns and contractions.

A medical transcriptionist must know when to edit (when it would not affect the dictator's meaning or style) and how to edit (how to transform the transcription into clear, concise and more logical expressions of the same information).

1-C   Basic Medical Transcription Tools

Medical transcriptionists use various forms of equipment and reference materials in their trade. Some basic equipment you may have at your work station, or the area in which you work, could include the following: **transcribers** (machines in which an audiocassette tape is used, and which typically have headphones for private listening and a footpedal so that hands can be made free for keying); **typewriters**; and **word processing equipment** (a screen on which typed characters are displayed, a keyboard, a printer, and a memory bank), which makes editing documents a great deal more simple than on a typewriter. See Unit 3 for a comprehensive list of medical transcription reference materials. However, the greatest tool that medical transcriptionists have at their fingertips is their collective intelligence—the knowledge gained over the many hours spent honing their skills.

The Medical Transcriber. The medical transcriber is essential to the medical transcriptionist. It is a machine that allows the transcriptionist to take oral dictation, decipher and encode it, and turn the spoken words into written material. The transcriber is the device that makes it possible to transform voice recordings into transcripts (printed documents).

Parts of the Transcriber. The audiocassette voice transcriber consists of a base (where the cassette is inserted), headphones and a footpedal. The transcriber usually has a speed control, a tone control and a volume control. Each transcriptionist can adjust these controls to fit his or her needs. For example, a beginning transcriptionist will frequently turn the speed to a low setting, so that the dictation can be heard at a slower rate than the actual manner in which the physician dictated. If the dictator's speech has a nasal tonality or a stuttering style, a change in the tone control may be necessary. Volume may also need to be controlled from dictator to dictator, as some physicians speak quite loudly, while others are difficult to hear. (See Figure 2.)

As with most cassette players, there are also play, stop, rewind and fast forward buttons on the base control board. These controls are useful when previewing or scanning tapes that have not yet been transcribed, or when the footpedals are lacking any of these controls. However, the footpedal should be primarily used for playing and rewinding the dictation.

Pictured in Figure 2 is a standard transcriber unit. In most cases, the play pedal is located on the right or in the center. In some cases, however, the play pedal is situated on the left side. There usually is a rewind pedal, either on the right or on the left. The fast forward pedal can be located either on the footpedal on the right, left, top or center, or, less frequently, on the base. Sometimes there is a footrest in the center section. Check the directions for use before beginning to transcribe. Directions for use of most footpedals: Push the right side of the footpedal to play, and the left side to rewind. Take your foot off the pedal to stop it from playing temporarily as you transcribe. Always listen to an earful or play just a few words more than you can transcribe, so you can continue keying as you take your foot off the play pedal. Press the play pedal to continue hearing dictation.

The Standard Cassette Transcriber. The most frequently used type of audiocassette transcriber, the **standard cassette transcriber**, uses standard audio tapes (3-15/16″ x 2-1/2″). These cassettes are commonly used in commercial audio recordings and with most types of portable and stereo cassette recorders and players. Hospitals generally use standard cassettes, although some physicians' offices and many clinics also use these models. The cassettes are sold everywhere from supermarkets and department stores to music specialty stores.

The Microcassette Transcriber. The transcriber that utilizes the smallest cassette tapes on the market today, the micro-sized audiocassette tapes (2″ x 1-1/4″), is the **microcassette transcriber**. Microcassettes are frequently used by physicians' offices and clinics because of their easy use and the fact that the dictating machines that accommodate them are hand-held, pocket-size models. The actual cassettes are also usually sold in supermarkets and department stores, as well as in business supply stores.

FIGURE 2   The Standard Transcriber

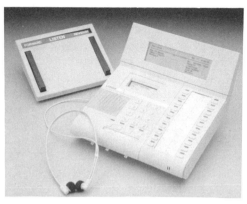

Photo Courtesy Of Lanier Voice Products

The Mini-Cassette Transcriber. The transcriber that employs a cassette tape size whose use is almost exclusively limited to transcribing machines is the **mini-cassette transcriber.** These mini-sized audio tapes are 2 3/16″ x 1 3/8″. This size audio tape is only slightly larger than the microcassette, but microcassette transcribers usually cannot accommodate mini-cassettes and vice versa. Mini-cassettes are frequently used by physicians' offices that have been in practice for many years (as the mini-cassette preceded the microcassette, and many physicians still continue to use and treasure their somewhat out-of-date mini-cassette dictating machines). Mini-cassettes are generally only sold in dictating specialty stores.

1-D   The Medical Transcription Environment

It is important to understand the **environment** in which a medical transcriptionist works, as many factors in transcribing and editing a physician's dictation depend on the physical proximity of the physician to the transcriptionist. If the physician can be easily contacted for questions and/or revisions, the transcriptionist may be able to transcribe more liberally. However, if the physician can only be contacted through a series of steps in a chain of command, then the transcriptionist must be more rigid and rule-adhering in transcribing the dictation.

As previously mentioned, medical transcriptionists work in hospitals, clinics, medical offices, medical transcription services and in their own homes. The chain of command is different for each of these settings, and you should be aware of them and the proximity of the transcriptionist to the physician in each case.

The flow chart that follows shows the hospital as a medical transcription environment.

In the hospital, the medical transcriptionist rarely has much direct contact with the dictating physician. The normal route of progress from dictation to transcription is as follows: The physician dictates a report, indicates to the medical staff office that the dictation has been made, and places it in a receptacle designated for medical transcription in the medical records department. The transcriptionist takes the dictation, transcribes it, prints it out if necessary, and places it in a designated location for completed reports. The report is then either charted to await the physician's perusal and signature, or placed in a designated area for completed medical transcription. Therefore, contact with the physician is limited. In the majority of instances, the physician and the transcriptionist do not make any direct contact and rely on the medical records department as an intermediary.

THE HOSPITAL
AS A MEDICAL TRANSCRIPTION ENVIRONMENT

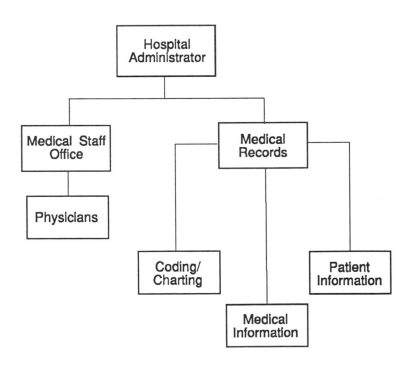

The flowchart that follows shows the medical office as a medical transcription environment.

THE MEDICAL OFFICE
AS A MEDICAL TRANSCRIPTION ENVIRONMENT

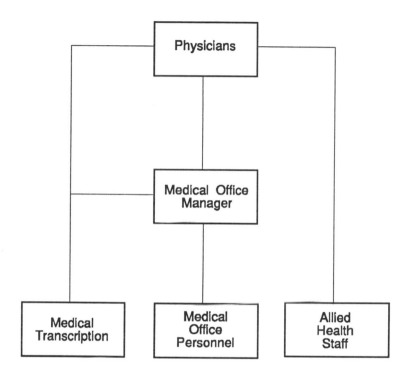

In the medical office, the medical transcriptionist usually has quite a bit of direct contact with the dictating physician. Sometimes the medical office manager may act as an intermediary, conveying messages from the transcriptionist to the physician, or the transcriptionist may go directly to the physician with questions or problems. The normal route of progress from dictation to transcription is as follows: The physician dictates a report and delivers it either to the medical office manager or directly to the transcriptionist. The transcriptionist takes the dictation, transcribes it, prints it out if necessary, and either gives it to the physician for signature or to the medical office manager for initial clearance.

The flowchart that follows shows the medical transcription service as a medical transcription environment.

THE MEDICAL TRANSCRIPTION SERVICE
AS A MEDICAL TRANSCRIPTION ENVIRONMENT

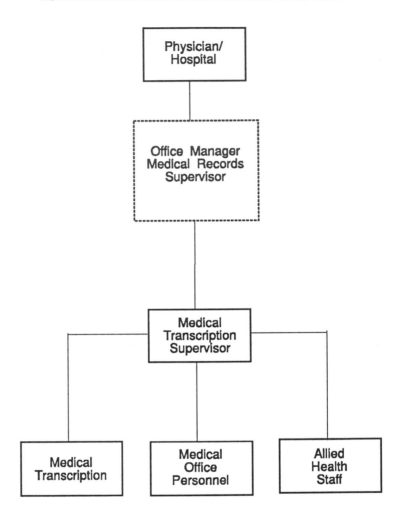

In the medical transcription service, the medical transcriptionist usually has no direct contact with the dictating physician. The normal route of progress from dictation to transcription is as follows: The physician dictates a report and delivers it either to the medical office manager/medical records supervisor or directly to the medical transcription supervisor at the medical transcription service. The transcriptionist takes the dictation, transcribes it, and gives it to either the proofer, who will proofread the report and print it out (in the previous two instances, the medical transcriptionist must proofread his or her own work), or to a clerk, who will print out the report and give it to the supervisor. After the supervisor's critique, the report goes back to the office manager or medical records, or directly back to the physician for signature.

Unit 2

Microcomputer Tools: An Introduction To Word Processing

Overview: Computerization is now a standard part of every major industry. Medical transcription is certainly no exception. In fact, computerized word processing (keyboarding and manipulating words, or generating written communication) has become an integral part of transcribing medical reports, letters and other correspondence. Most hospitals and many physicians' offices incorporate computerization into their daily routines. Computerization is used in everything from bookkeeping to appointment scheduling to medical records production. If you are unfamiliar with it, computerization may seem frightening or intimidating to you at first. But with just a little familiarization with the components and uses of computer equipment, you will quickly be thinking of your microcomputer word processor as one of the best pieces of equipment you have ever used. Not only will you learn to like working with computers, you will also realize how limited the functions of a standard typewriter are in comparison.

2-A   What Is Word Processing?

Word processing is a clerical support system involving the use of technology, proper procedures and trained personnel in creating, compiling and maneuvering a body of written material. Creating documents has always been rather simple: either handwriting or typewriting was used to generate text. A major problem with handwritten text is that it can be hard to decipher and is not uniform. A problem with typewritten text is that it is not saved and the original is the only permanent record. Compiling and maneuvering the information is even more difficult with hand- and type-writing: if a change needs to be made, it needs to be erased, corrected with opaquing fluid (white-out), or manually removed in some other way; if something needs to be added or moved, the entire text or a portion thereof usually has to be cut, copied, pasted and/or rekeyed.

The word processor is able to perform the tasks of creating, compiling and maneuvering text without the use of scissors, new paper, erasers or correction fluid. Another feature of the word processor is that, unlike the typewriter, it can also save an entire document or a group of documents. This data storage ability makes it possible for you to begin working on a document, save it, retrieve it, and work on it again at a later time. Also, multiple copies of the document can be made at any time without the use of reproductive copiers. Therefore, word-processed documents are more permanent, flexible and easily manipulated than typewritten or handwritten documents.

2-B   What Are Microcomputers?

Most computers used in offices and hospitals today are truly microcomputers, or computers that are quite a bit smaller than their predecessors, which took up large portions of any office and were cumbersome and extremely complicated to use. Microcomputers usually use disks or diskettes to store information, instead of reel-to-reel tapes or audiocassette tapes, as some of the older computer models use.

You may hear the terms microcomputer and word processor often inter-changed; however, the fact is that word processing is actually only one of the many uses of microcomputers. Word processing programs, such as Word-Perfect® (which you will find a brief guide to in Appendix A), WordStar®, Displaywrite® and MicroSoft Word®, are software programs that contain instructions, procedures and formats for making keyboarding easier than on a regular typewriter. Unlike a typewriter, most word processing programs allow you to do such things as print in bold type and double underlined, print in different type styles (fonts), print graphics such as designs and charts, and do a variety of other functions that would be difficult or impossible to do on a regular typewriter. Most microcomputers, in addition to word processing, also perform such other tasks as making databases, creating spreadsheets, formulating com-puter programs, and a host of other chores under control of the disk operating system (this is briefly explained in Appendix A, as you might need to also use DOS commands when word processing). There are, however, on the market today microcomputers that exclusively use word processing programs and perform word processing functions, and cannot be used for other tasks. In this text we will use the terms microcomputer and word processor interchangeably, as we assume that the majority of your work on the microcomputer will, in fact, be word processing.

Figure 3 shows microcomputer hardware and software. Become familiar with these terms and parts of the microcomputer, as you will certainly encounter them many times in your career as a medical transcriptionist.

2-C   Parts of the Microcomputer: Hardware

Pictured in Figure 3 are the parts of the microcomputer. The **monitor** is the component of the computer that is known as the screen. On the monitor, you view your work as you key it, just as you would on a piece of paper when working with a typewriter. In addition to displaying the text as you key it, a monitor may also be capable of displaying graphics (pictures). Types of moni-

FIGURE 3   A Microprocessor with a Monitor, Central Processing Unit, Keyboard, and Printer

tors include MGA (monochrome graphics adaptor), CGA (color graphics adaptor), EGA (enhanced graphics adaptor), and VGA (video graphics array).

The **keyboard** you are already undoubtedly familiar with. This is the part of the computer on which you key, or type, characters. There are two major types of keyboards: the standard IBM 10-function keyboard and the enhanced IBM 12-function keyboard (pictured in Figure 4). Most of the keys are quite similar to the keys of a regular typewriter. However, in addition, you will note some special keys not found on a typewriter, such as the **Esc** or escape key; the **Ins** and **Del** keys, or insert and delete keys; the **F1** through **F12** keys, or the function keys; the **Ctrl** and **Alt** keys, or control and alternate keys; and the keys with arrows on them, or the cursor keys. The escape key usually performs specialized tasks that vary with each separate word processing program. The insert key allows you to either key while inserting new characters without replacing the old ones or key while replacing existing characters with new characters. The delete key is similar to the regular backspace key; however, it deletes characters to the right or in front of where your place holder (or cursor) is instead of deleting behind or to the left, as backspace does.

The function keys usually have specialized tasks, or functions, that vary with each word processor. Some of these functions could include underlining, making characters bold or italicized, spell checking, etc. The control and alternate keys usually allow the function keys or other keys to have a third and a fourth level of functioning (the first level is the key by itself; the second level is the key with the Shift key depressed).

The cursor keys move your **cursor** (usually a flashing bar that tells you where your next character will be keyed) around on a page or in a document. With the cursor arrow keys, you can move your cursor to the left, to the right, and up and down. You can also move the cursor a great distance at a time, such as an entire page or to the very beginning or very end of a document, no matter how many pages it may contain.

FIGURE 4   Pictured are the standard IBM 10-function keyboard (above) and the enhanced 12-function keyboard (below).

Lastly, there is the Enter key, which performs the same task as the Return key on a regular typewriter.

Another part of the microcomputer is the **central processing unit (CPU)**. This is the brain of the microcomputer. The diskettes you use for your word processing program are inserted into the holes, or drives, of the CPU. The drives contain a slot, into which the diskette is put, and a lever or door, which when closed informs the CPU that the diskette is ready to be looked at, or read. There are several types of microcomputer disk configurations, but the most frequently used are either a dual floppy disk drive or a hard drive/floppy disk drive combination. The configuration of the CPU is typically to have either two floppy disk drives (drive A and drive B, which are symbolized A: and B:) or a hard disk drive and a floppy disk drive (drive C and drive A, symbolized C: and A:). (Note: Do not put diskettes in or take diskettes out when the red light next to the door is on. When the red light is on, the disk is being read, and moving the disk can damage it.) The CPU also contains a buffer, or a small memory area that is separate from the diskettes. The buffer allows you to perform certain functions without having the main operating system disk inserted and also remembers certain things without you having saved them. The switches that turn the computer off and on are also generally located on the CPU. After turning the computer on, you need to put a floppy diskette containing DOS in the main disk drive (usually in drive A:), or you must have a copy of DOS saved on your hard disk drive if you are using one, to actually make the computer ready to read and write to diskettes. After entering the date and time (if this is asked of you when you put the diskette in the drive and turn it on), you will see a prompt. The process of turning on the CPUs power supply and getting to the prompt on the monitor is called **booting up.**

A part of the microcomputer that is essential to the full use of its word processing abilities, but is not usually necessary to operate the microcomputer, is the **printer.** The printer makes a hard copy (paper copy) of any data you designate to be printed. Microcomputer printers are usually either dot matrix printers (9-pin dot matrix printers print only in dot matrix form; whereas 24-pin dot matrix printers print in dot matrix quality or near letter quality form, where you cannot see the individual dots), letter quality printers (these printers use daisywheels, and usually print in identical quality to standard typewriters, but cannot usually support graphics or different type styles), and laser jet printers (printers with high resolution used to print high-quality, publishable characters and graphics).

2-D   Software, Diskettes and Disk Drives for the Microcomputer

Software. Microcomputer program packages are known as software. A word processing program, such as WordPerfect, is a type of software. The software is made up of **disks** or **diskettes** (which contain the programming), instructional and reference manuals, and materials such as **templates** (paper or plastic overlays for the keys that explain the function of the keys, especially the function keys, and other uses of the keyboard for a particular software program). Consult the documentation that comes with your specific word processing package for in-depth instructions on how to use the program. Pictured in Figure 5 are both the 51/4-inch and the 31/2-inch diskette.

Diskettes. There are disks that are external to the microcomputer (floppy diskettes or nonflexible diskettes) and disks that are internal to the microcomputer (stationary metallic hard disks, or Winchester disks). Floppy diskettes, shown below in Figure 5, are flexible disks made of mylar plastic coated with a magnetic oxide and enclosed in a square plastic case. The surface of the mylar disk contains concentric rings, called tracks, which can be allocated like portions of a filing cabinet (filing drawers). The tracks can be further divided into sections called sectors.

When you **format** a diskette, or prepare it to receive data, you are defining the sectors. Once the sectors have been defined, the diskette is ready to receive

FIGURE 5   Pictured are the 5¼-inch diskette and the 3½-inch diskette.

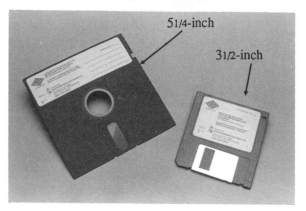

data. You can save data to the diskette using your word processing program, a disk operating system, or another computer program.

The data in each sector is also broken down into units. These units of data are called **bytes**, spaces reserved for information. The byte's information could be a single character, a space or group of spaces, or a specific command for the computer to execute. Floppy diskettes come in two sizes and have various storage capacities: 51/4-inch floppy diskettes are available with capacities of 360,000 bytes and 1.2 megabytes, and 31/2-inch floppy diskettes are available with capacities of 700,000 bytes and 1.44 megabytes. Figure 5 shows these two diskette sizes. Following are some common byte conversion factors:

1 byte = approximately 0.67 information pieces (characters or character spaces)

1 character = approximately 1.5 bytes

1 byte = 8 bits (the language computer information is written in, in 0's and 1's)

1 kilobyte (1 KB or Kb) = 1024 bytes

1 megabyte (1 MB or Mb) = 1,048,576 bytes

Any data that you use is moved to the disks by magnetic impulses produced by an electromagnet in the disk drive, called a read-write head. The read-write head performs two major functions: reading and writing. Reading from a diskette is when the microcomputer looks at programmed data on the disk and tells you something about that data. Writing to a diskette is when the microcomputer allows you to add new information onto a disk or change existing data on a disk. As the data is read or written, the drive containing the diskette is spinning at a high rate of speed. This is why it is important not to move the diskette when the drive is spinning (the drive is spinning every time the red light is on).

Each diskette also contains a directory system. Every diskette has at least a main directory, the main section where all files are stored unless they are stored in a subdirectory. To further organize the data on your diskette, you can create subdirectories, which are sometimes simply called directories (See Appendix A for further information on creating [sub]directories). The subdirectories tell the drive the sector in which to look for any particular data. The directory system is similar to the file drawers in a filing cabinet. Each directory, or file cabinet, can also contain several files, just like manila folders in a filing cabinet. The file names are the names of your documents. The files are the smallest organizational component, besides the bytes, on the diskette.

The most commonly used diskettes are flexible, or floppy, and are 5¼ inches in size, although smaller, nonflexible diskettes that are 3½ inches in size are becoming more widespread in use. Preprogrammed diskettes contain information you need in order to use the word processing program. See the individual reference materials that were purchased with the software package for further information on how to use each program's diskettes.

Disk Drives. Disk drives are what control, or drive, the operation of a disk or diskette. When using a dual floppy disk drive, it is necessary to always have the diskettes for the program handy. You will have to alternate the insertion of the program diskettes with other blank diskettes, on which you store your own documents. All blank diskettes need to be formatted in order to use them (see Appendix A for specific instructions on formatting).

The other most common (and greater capacity) disk drive system is the hard disk drive (sometimes called a Winchester disk drive). The hard disk drive system also contains at least one floppy disk drive, into which you insert floppy diskettes and should generally use to save new information. The hard disk drive itself consists of at least one round metal plate coated with a magnetic oxide, similar to the floppy diskettes. The hard disk drive is contained inside a cabinet within the microcomputer. Unlike the floppy disk, the hard disk may be divided, or partitioned, into more than one drive. Each partition can have a different drive name (C:, D:, E:, & F:), but usually only one partition (C:) is formatted (or preformatted by the manufacturer before you purchase it) for use. The hard disk drive usually has a minimum of 20,000,000 bytes (20 MB, or megabytes) or more of total storage capacity. Do not confuse disk storage capacity with the size or amount of CPU working memory. The CPU memory (often called random access memory, or RAM) consists of an array of semiconductor chips and is where the operating system and word processor programs are placed for quick access. Typical RAM sizes are 512 and 640 KB.

When using a hard/floppy disk drive, you can usually copy the word processing program(s) you will use onto the hard disk, and then use the floppy disk drive for the blank formatted diskettes you will use for saving new information. (See your microcomputer's operating manual and the word processing program's operating manuals for further information on this.) You may also allocate space on the hard disk on which you may save documents, but even though the hard disk contains several millions of bytes of space, its storage capacity is not limitless; therefore, most people save the majority of their documents on diskettes.

2-E   Diskette Handling

Be careful when using diskettes (see Figure 6). They are extremely fragile. Follow these precautions when handling floppy diskettes:

1.   Touch only the top of the diskette, near the label, and touch only where the plastic is covering the actual mylar disk. NEVER TOUCH THE MYLAR DISK.

2.   Place the diskette in a paper holder when it is not in use.

3.   Never allow liquid, dust, ashes, fingers, magnets or magnetic devices, electric machines, electronic appliances, telephones, or radio-controlled devices to touch or come in contact with the mylar disk surface, as they could alter the disk's magnetic impressions.

4.   While studies have shown that floppy diskettes are not usually damaged by x-ray scanning machines such as are used in courtrooms and airports,

FIGURE 6   Basic diskette handling precautions are: (a) never touch the mylar coated disk;
▬▬▬▬▬   (b) never bend or fold the diskette; (c) never allow the diskette to come into
              contact with magnetic devices.

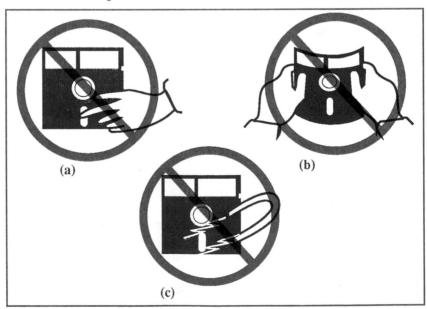

(a)   (b)

(c)

it is advisable to have floppy diskettes checked by hand or otherwise not be taken through the scanning machine.

5. Never leave a diskette in a drive slot when turning off the power supply to the microcomputer. Sudden surges in the power supply can cause the disk drive's read-write head to crash against the diskette, making the diskette unusable. Only put a diskette in a disk drive before turning on the power supply when the microcomputer system does not have an autoboot feature (the diskette's function is to boot up, or turn on, the microcomputer as soon as the system can read a disk containing DOS).

6. Keep the environment surrounding your diskettes at a temperature between 40-125 degrees Fahrenheit (10-52 degrees Celsius). It is advisable to keep your microcomputer system in a cool, well-ventilated area. Also, do not block the ventilation holes on the outside of the CPU.

7. Do not press a ballpoint pen or pencil directly against the covering of a diskette when writing upon it. Try to mark labels before placing them on the diskette cover, or use a felt-tip or light-touch pen when writing on the diskette cover is necessary.

8. Never bend, fold, crease, staple, smash, tear or cut the mylar disk or its cover.

Unit 3

Use of Reference Materials

Overview: Some additional important tools that a medical transcriptionist uses daily are reference materials, such as dictionaries, texts, indices, word lists, and other books and written materials that can aid a transcriptionist in choosing the correct word and correctly spelling that word. The following are some helpful and frequently used reference materials, which you should add to your personal library over time (see Figure 7):.

3-A   Reference Book Types

Medical Dictionary. Look up words in this book in overall alphabetical order. Look up double words (such as Hemophilus influenzae) by either first or last word. Gives complete definition of all words. *Value: Great*

Physician's Desk Reference. Look up drug names in one of the following sections: the manufacturer's index (by maker's name), the product name index (combined brand and generic names, without differentiation), the product category index (systemic use of drug, e.g., antipruritic), the generic and chemical name index *Value: Moderate*

FIGURE 7   Reference Materials

(does not include brand names), or the product identification section (identification of drug by physical appearance). Also includes drug indications, precautions, and dosage and overdosage information.

Transcription Style/Handbook. Look up questions you might have about how to use abbreviations, numerals, capitalization, punctuation types, etc. Look up questions by various categories. Includes sections on often misspelled/misused words.

Value: Great

Drug Index/ Catalogue. Look up drugs by name only. You can determine if the drug is generic or not based on the book's print or type. Also includes brief pharmacological compounds and uses. Gives a list of common brand names after generic listings.

Value: Great

Medical Word Book. There are two major types of medical word books. In one type, the systemic word listing guide, you look up a word in the section dealing with its associated system (i.e., for retinitis you would look in the ophthalmology section). In the other type, the alphabetical word listing guide, you look up a word in its overall alphabetical order. These word books may also contain plate diagrams of certain systems and a small number of most frequently used drug names, surgical words, general medical words and abbreviations.

Value: Great

Medical Specialty Wordbook. A must for the transcriptionist who transcribes specialty medical reports, such as operative or pathology reports. Look up a word either in overall alphabetical order or by general type of instrument, operation or item (i.e., for McBurney incision, you could look under McBurney or incision) in the surgical word book or by specific disease name in the pathology word book.

Value: Moderate

Grammar Reference Book. Look up punctuation, grammar usage, spelling rules and mechanics such as capitalization, numbers and italics first in the table of contents or index, or on the endsheets in the back of the book, and then on the page(s) to which it directs you.

Value: Great

3-B   Recommended Reference Materials

Dictionaries:

- *Dorland's Illustrated Medical Dictionary*
- *The New Roget's Thesaurus of the English Language in Dictionary Form*
- *Encyclopedia and Dictionary of Medicine, Nursing and Allied Health*
- *Stedman's Medical Dictionary*

- *Taber's Cyclopedic Medical Dictionary*
- *Webster's Ninth New Collegiate Dictionary*
- *Webster's Third New International Dictionary of the English Language, Unabridged*

Word Books:

- *A Word Book in Pathology and Laboratory Medicine*
- *The Medical & Health Sciences Word Book*
- *Medical Phrase Index*
- *The Medical Word Book*
- *The Surgical Word Book*

Drug Catalogues/Indices:

- *American Drug Index*
- *Physicians' Desk Reference*

Grammar Handbooks:

- *The Little, Brown Handbook*
- *Reference Manual*

Word Processing References:

- *The ABC's of MS-DOS*
- *Using WordPerfect 5.1, Special Edition*
- *WordPerfect for IBM Personal Computers*

Other Medical References:

- *Accreditation Manual for Hospitals*
- *Contemporary Medical Office Procedures*
- *Current Medical Terminology*
- *DeGowin & DeGowin's Bedside Diagnostic Examination*
- *Forrest General Medical Center: Advanced Medical Terminology and Transcription Course*
- *Getting a Job in Health Care*
- *H & P: A Nonphysician's Guide*
- *Hillcrest Medical Center: Beginning Medical Transcription Course*
- *The Language of Medicine*

- *Medical Abbreviations: 5500 Conveniences at the Expense of Communications and Safety*
- *Medical Abbreviations Handbook*
- *Medical and Dental Associates, P.C.: Insurance Forms Preparation*
- *Medical Office Practice*
- *Medical Pegboard Procedures*
- *The Merck Manual*
- *The Modern Medical Office: A Reference Manual*
- *MS-DOS Version 3, Basic Concepts and Features*
- *Psychology: Studying the Behavior of People*
- *Style Guide for Medical Transcription*
- *Terminology for Allied Health Professionals*

Part Two

Medical Transcription Formats

Unit 4

Types of Medical Reports and Formats

Overview: When transcribing medical reports, it is essential to know the proper format. Because physicians and other dictators do not always break down a report into its correct sections, and sometimes fail to specify the report title, it is imperative for a transcriptionist to be able to identify sections of various types of reports, as well as know how to transcribe them. A basic explanation of the main types of medical report formats follows.

4-A   Main Types of Medical Reports

The six basic types of medical reports are:

History and Physical

Operative Note

Consultation Report

Pathology Report

Radiology Report

Discharge Summary

4-B   Brief Explanations of Each Type of Report

1. **History and Physical.** This is the report generated by the admitting physician, the resident or the hospital internist upon formal admission of a patient to the hospital. This report focuses on the patient's history that led to the present illness; the patient's past, social and family histories, if contributory; the review of systems; and the physical findings the patient exhibits on examination. Note: There is an important difference between the history of the present illness (HPI), the review of systems and the physical examination. The HPI is basically the patient's oral history given to the doctor of related matters such as the onset and duration of the illness, any precipitating factors, any previous hospitalizations or treatment for this particular illness, any allergies or chronic

illnesses, and a current immunization record. The review of systems is, again, an oral history, but it is different in that it is an account of the patient's history related to specific systems and organs, such as headaches, heart palpitations, pains in the toes, etc., from a historical point of view. The physical examination is not historical; it is the physician's tactile evaluation of the patient's systems and organs, e.g., the patient's vital signs, heart auscultation, reflex examination, etc.

2.   **Consultation Report.** This report is requested of a specialist physician by the patient's primary or attending physician. The patient's attending physician requests a consultation because he or she would like a second opinion on a particular problem or diagnosis regarding the patient's problem. This report focuses on the dictating physician's (consultant's) impression and recommendations for treatment. This report is addressed from (dictated by) the consultant and it is addressed to the attending physician. This report usually contains a date of consultation, the reason for consultation, physical and laboratory evaluation of the patient, and the consultant's impression and recommendations. There may also be a complimentary close at the end, such as "Thank you for this referral," and to include this in the typed report is proper procedure.

3.   **Operative Note.** This report describes a surgical procedure. The report is usually dictated by the surgeon or an assistant. The focus of this report is the actual description of the operative procedure. Usually also dictated in this report are the preoperative and postoperative diagnoses, the name of the surgeon, the title and date of the procedure, the indications for surgery, the surgical findings, and the actual description of the surgery, called the procedure. There is also usually a sponge count and an amount of estimated blood loss, and the report typically ends with the patient being taken to the recovery room. Special note: If a medical word ends in -ectomy, -plasty, -pexy, -otomy, or -rrhaphy, the word probably relates to a surgical procedure.

4.   **Pathology Report.** This diagnostic report describes the pathological or disease-related findings of a sample of tissue taken. The tissue samples can be taken during surgery, a biopsy, a special procedure, or an autopsy. The autopsy is also a special type of pathology report that is requested by the attending physician or a coroner when the cause of a patient's death is in doubt. The pathology report is dictated by a pathologist. This report focuses on the gross and microscopic findings (cytology and histology), and the pathological diagnosis. An important note here is that the pathology report is not synonymous with the laboratory data; the pathology report is a separate report of any disease findings usually limited to tissue, while laboratory data are usually information regarding body fluids. Also, the laboratory data section is only part of another type of report (e.g., the history and physical or the discharge summary) and does not stand on its own.

5.   **Radiology Report.** This report describes a diagnostic procedure using radio waves or other forms of radiation. Some major diagnostic procedures are roentgenograms (basic x-rays), CT scans (computerized tomography scans), MRI scans (magnetic resonance imaging scans), nuclear medicine procedures (such as thyroid scans and bone scans with an injection or infusion of radioactive contrast), fluoroscopic examinations, or any other visually recorded procedures performed upon the patient to make a diagnosis. The report is dictated by the radiologist. The focus of the report is the radiologist's impression. Special note: If a medical word ends in -scopy or -graphy, it probably indicates that it involves a radiologic procedure.

6.   **Discharge Summary.** This report summarizes the hospitalization of the patient. The report describes the reason the patient was admitted to the hospital, the patient's history, and a review of the events that occurred during his or her hospitalization. This report focuses on the hospital course and the discharge diagnoses. The report, also called a dismissal summary or a summary of hospitalization, can also include the history of the present illness and other histories such as the family history and social history, the physical examination, laboratory data, follow-up instructions, discharge medication, and the patient's condition on discharge and prognosis.

In addition to the above six main types of reports, other reports are often dictated on a patient, including the emergency room note, the psychiatric history, interim reports, the autopsy, and special procedures that receive the attention of an entire report, such as cardiac catheterization and esophagogastroduodenoscopy. Follow the Discharge Summary format as a general guideline for these reports, and include the titles of these reports in the report's header or footer.

4-C   Turnaround Time for Medical Reports

Turnaround time is the time it takes for the report to be dictated, transcribed and signed or verified by the physician. Hospital reports are usually divided into three classes in terms of turnaround time: stat, current and old. Stat reports, such as radiology reports and pathology reports, usually have a turnaround time of 12 hours or less, as the report is probably required for other evaluation and treatment to be performed on the patient. Current reports, such as history and physical reports, consultations and operative notes, usually have a turnaround time of 24 hours. Old reports, such as discharge summaries and emergency room notes, are usually not necessary to have in the patient's file before other measures can be taken in terms of his or her treatment, so the turnaround time on these reports is usually 72 hours. Some hospital medical records departments have different turnaround times, some longer and some shorter, but generally speaking, if the physician fails to meet the established turnaround deadline for dictating a report he or she may have the privilege to admit patients to the hospital suspended. Likewise, if the report is dictated on time and fails to be transcribed in a timely manner, the medical records department can be held liable for any legal action resulting from the patient's medical file not being complete.

It is important for the medical transcriptionist to be aware of turnaround times for specific reports, and to meet the proper deadlines and be prompt in the transcription of all dictation. Failure to meet deadlines could result in legal problems for the medical records department and/or disciplinary action being taken against the medical transcriptionist.

4-D   Specific Report Formats

Use the following formats as guidelines for transcribing hospital medical records. Keep in mind, however, that these formats are not necessarily the standard format for all medical facilities; some hospitals may have different formats, so always consult the institution you are transcribing for before actual transcription of the dictation.

Remember the following points about formats when transcribing reports:

1.   Always consult the physician or medical institution for the proper format to use.

2.   If the institution you are transcribing for permits, try to include section headings when none are dictated.

3.   If a section is omitted by the dictator, leave the section out; do not include the section simply because the format dictates it should be there.

4.   Some offices and hospitals use different methods for noting patient identification that is placed on the medical record. The following format examples include only the patient's name and hospital number; however, some institutions may include such varied information as the patient's room number, address, phone number, age, religion, sex, marital status, diagnosis, etc. Please be aware of this, and include all information that the particular institution you are transcribing for requires. If certain information is not required (as it might infringe upon patient confidentiality), however, do not include it in the report, even if dictated.

5.   If someone other than the attending physician dictates the report, this is usually indicated somewhere in the report. In the examples that follow, this information, where applicable, is included in the footer. In the History and Physical Report and the Discharge Summary, if dictated by someone other than the attending physician, there are two signature lines —one for the attending physician and one for the dictating physician or other dictator. (In the Operative Report, Consultation Report, Radiology Report and Pathology Report, since these reports are almost always

dictated by someone other than the attending physician, there is only one signature line—one for the dictator.)

6. In the formats that follow, and in several hospital formats used nation-wide, the abbreviations "D:" and "T:" are used. These abbreviations stand for the dates of dictation and transcription.

Specific general examples of the six basic medical reports follow. Figures 8 and 9 demonstrate where to place patient information in reports. Figures 10, 11, 12, 13, 14 and 15 demonstrate the formats for the six major types of medical reports, with the patient information located in the footer. Always keep in mind, however, that these formats are only guidelines, and each hospital may employ its own specific formats for reports.

FIGURE 8   Medical Report with Patient Information in Header

REPORT TITLE

Patient Name: Xxxxx Xxxxx   Hospital Number: XXXXX
Attending Physician: Xxxx Xxxxx, M.D.   Room Number: XXX
Date of Admission: XX/XX/XX

HISTORY OF PRESENT ILLNESS: xxxxxxxxxxxxxxxxxxxxxxxxxxxxxxxxxxxxxxx
xxxxxxxxxxxxxxxxxxxxxxxxxxxxxxxxxxxxxxxxxxxxxxxxxxxxxxxxxxxxxxxxxxxx
xxxxxxxxxxxxxxxxxxxxxxxxxxxxxxxxxxxxxxxxxxxxxxxxxxxxxxxxxxxxxx
xxxxxxxxxxxxxxxxx.

Past History: Xxxxxxxxxxxxxxxxxxxxxxxxxxxxxxxxxxxxxxxxxxxxxxxxxx
xxxxxxxxxxxxxxxxxxxxxxxxxxxxxxxxxxxxxxxxxxxxxxxxxxxx.

Social History: Xxxxxxxxxxxxxxxxxxxxxxxxxxxxxxxxxxxxxxxxxxxxxxxxx
xxxxxxxxxxxxxxxxxxxxxxxxxxxxxxxxxxxxxx.

Family History: X xxxxxxxxxxxxxxxxxxxxxxxxxxxxxxxxxxxxxxxxxxxxxxxx
xxxxxxxxxxxxxxxxxxxxxxxxxxxxxxxxxxxxxxxx.

REVIEW OF SYSTEMS:
Xxxxxx: Xxxxxxxxxxxxxxxxxxxxxxxxxxxxxxxxxxxxxxxxxxxxxxxxxxxxxxx
Xxxxxxxxxxx: Xxxxxxxxxxxxxxxxxxxx xxxxxxxxxxxxxxxxxxxxxxxxxxxxxx

PHYSICAL EXAMINATION:
xxxxxxxxxxxxxxxxxxxxxxxxxxxxxxxxxxxxxxxxxxxxxxxxxxxxxxxxxxxxxxxxxxxx
xxxxxxxxxxxxxxxxxx.
Xxxxxxxxx: Xxxxxxxxxxxxxxxxxxxxxxxxxxxxxxxxxxxxxxxxxxxx.

                                    _____
                                    Xxxxx Xxxxx, M.D.

D: (Date of dictation) XX/XX/XX
T: (Date of transcription) XX/XX/XX
XX/xx (Physician's initials in capitals and/or transcriptionist's initials in lowercase)

FIGURE 9   Medical Report with Patient Information in Footer

MERCY MEDICAL CENTER
300 Main Street
Denver, CO 80201

REPORT TITLE

HISTORY OF PRESENT ILLNESS: xxxxxxxxxxxxxxxxxxxxxxxxxxxxxxxxxxxxxxx
xxxxxxxxxxxxxxxxxxxxxxxxxxxxxxxxxxxxxxxxxxxxxxxxxxxxxxxxxxxxxxxxxxxx
xxxxxxxxxxxxxxxxxxxxxxxxxxxxxxxxxxxxxxxxxxxxxxxxxxxxxxxxxxxxxx
xxxxxxxxxxxxxxxxx.

Past History: Xxxxxxxxxxxxxxxxxxxxxxxxxxxxxxxxxxxxxxxxxxxxxxxxxx
xxxxxxxxxxxxxxxxxxxxxxxxxxxxxxxxxxxxxxxx.

Social History: Xxxxxxxxxxxxxxxxxxxxxxxxxxxxxxxxxxxxxxxxxxxxxxxxx
xxxxxxxxxxxxxxxxxxxxxxxxxxxxxxxxxxxxxxx.

Family History: Xxxxxxxxxxxxxxxxxxxxxxxxxxxxxxxxxxxxxxxxxxxxxxxxxx
xxxxxxxxxxxxxxxxxxxxxxxxxxxxxxxxxxxxxxxxxxxxx.

REVIEW OF SYSTEMS:
Xxxxxx: Xxxxxxxxxxxxxxxxxxxxxxxxxxxxxxxxxxxxxxxxxxxxxxxxxxxxxxx.
Xxxxxxxxxxx: Xxxxxxxxxxxxxxxxxxxx xxxxxxxxxxxxxxxxxxxxxxxxxxxxxx

PHYSICAL EXAMINATION:
xxxxxxxxxxxxxxxxxxxxxxxxxxxxxxxxxxxxxxxxxxxxxxxxxxxxxxxxxxxxxxxxxxxx
xxxxxxxxxxxxxxxxxxxxxxxxxxx.
Xxxxxxxxx: Xxxxxxxxxxxxxxxxxxxxxxxxxxxxxxxxxxxxxxxxxxxx.

                                    _____
                                    Xxxxx Xxxxx, M.D.

ATTENDING PHYSICIAN's NAME   PATIENT's NAME HOSPITAL#

D: (Date of dictation) XX/XX/XX
T: (Date of transcription) XX/XX/XX
XX/xx (Physician's initials in capitals and/or transcriptionist's initials in lowercase)

REPORT TITLE

FIGURE 10: History and Physical Report

MERCY MEDICAL CENTER
300 Main Street
Denver, CO 80201

DATE OF ADMISSION: 10/02/XX

CHIEF COMPLAINT: Difficulty breathing.

HISTORY OF PRESENT ILLNESS: The patient is a 32-year-old, white, widowed woman who comes
in to the hospital complaining of dyspnea. She has been having these symptoms for over one
month now. The patient was told in her childhood that she exhibited some asthmatic
symptoms, although she has never been formally treated for same.

Past History: She had a tonsillectomy and adenoidectomy at age 12.

Social History: She is widowed; her husband died two years ago.

Family History: Noncontributory.

REVIEW OF SYSTEMS:
Head, eyes, ears, nose and throat: She has a history of having upper respiratory tract
infections every year. No throat pain. There is a history of a tonsilloadenoidectomy.
Chest: She has had no chest pain.
Gastrointestinal: Negative.
Extremities: Negative.
Neurologic: Negative.

PHYSICAL EXAMINATION:
General: She is a well-developed, well-nourished, white female. She is well dressed.
Vital signs: Temperature 36 degrees Celsius, respirations 24, pulse 78 and blood pressure
128/80. She is 5'6" tall. Her weight is 165 pounds.
Head, eyes, ears, nose and throat: Normocephalic and atraumatic. Pupils equal, round and
reactive to light and accommodation. Right pinna: There is some minimal swelling and edema
around the ear lobe; it is nontender. Nose: Mild rhinitis. The throat is clear.

CONTINUED

JOHN DOE, M.D.   SMITH, HARRIET #123456-7
D&T: 10/02/XX | 10/04/XX | DR/mt
Dictated by: Doc Residente, D.O.

HISTORY AND PHYSICAL

■■■■■
FIGURE 10 (continued): History and Physical Report

Page 2

Neck: Supple and nontender. There is no adenopathy or nuchal rigidity.
Chest: There are rales and rhonchi on expiration. Breath sounds are shallow.
Abdomen: Soft and nontender. Active bowel sounds. There is no hepatosplenomegaly.
Musculoskeletal: Negative.
Neurologic: Patellar reflexes are 2+. Deep tendon reflexes are 2+ bilaterally. No
Babinskis. Normal motor and sensory exam.
Skin: Mucous membranes are moist. There is good axillary sweat.

IMPRESSION:
1. Dyspnea.
2. Asthma.
3. Rule out pulmonary embolus.

PLAN:
Admit the patient to 2-North. Place the patient on a bronchodilator. Dr. Lopez,
pulmonologist, will consult in the morning.

                                        _____
                                        John Doe, M.D.
                                        Attending Physician

                                        _____
                                        Doc Residente, D.O.
                                        Dictating Physician

JOHN DOE, M.D.   SMITH, HARRIET #123456-7
D&T: 10/02/XX | 10/03/XX | DR/mt
Dictated by: Doc Residente, D.O.

HISTORY AND PHYSICAL

FIGURE 11   Consultation Report

MERCY MEDICAL CENTER
300 Main Street
Denver, CO 80201

DATE OF CONSULTATION: 10/03/XX

REASON FOR CONSULTATION: Dyspnea and asthma, rule out other pulmonary etiology.

CONSULTING PHYSICIAN: Gloria B. Lopez, M.D., Pulmonology

ATTENDING PHYSICIAN: John Doe, M.D.

The chart and pertinent physical findings have been reviewed. A chest x-ray was taken the morning after admission and showed a possible pulmonary embolus. Examination under fluoroscopy was performed, and it was positive for poor capillary filling and showed a plug that had been forced into a smaller one, thus obstructing the circulation. Pulmonary studies revealed the patient to have decreased lung capacity, a pulse oximetry of 88% and a high FEV to FVC ratio.   ·

The probable diagnosis at this time is acute asthma and pulmonary embolism, causing dyspnea and poor pulmonary circulation.

My recommendation is for a pulmonary angiogram and placement of a catheter. Thank you for your referral. I will follow this patient with you.

                                        _____

                                        Gloria B. Lopez, M.D.
                                        Pulmonology Department

JOHN DOE, M.D.   SMITH, HARRIET #123456-7
D&T: 10/03/XX | 10/04/XX | LM/mt
Dictated by: Gloria B. Lopez, M.D.

CONSULTATION REPORT

FIGURE 12: Operative Report

MERCY MEDICAL CENTER
300 Main Street
Denver, CO 80201

PREOPERATIVE DIAGNOSIS: Rule out pulmonary embolus.

POSTOPERATIVE DIAGNOSIS: Same.

SURGEON: Ima Cutter, M.D.

FIRST ASSISTANT: Sally Fingers, M.D.

OPERATIONS PERFORMED: 1.   Right brachial cutdown.
                      2.   Pulmonary angiogram.
                      3.   Placement of a Swan-Ganz catheter.

PROCEDURE: Under 2% Xylocaine local anesthesia and a Betadine prep, an incision was made over the right antecubital vein, and a #9 arterial catheter was advanced from the right antecubital area to the right pulmonary artery. Right pulmonary angiography was then done. Following this, a guide wire was placed. The arterial catheter was placed in the left main pulmonary artery, the guide wire was removed, and a left pulmonary angiogram was done. The catheter was then removed, and a Swan-Ganz catheter was advanced from the antecubital vein to the pulmonary artery. Pulmonary artery pressure was 21/8 and the pulmonary capillary wedge mean was approximately 5. The Swan-Ganz catheter was then removed.

The patient tolerated the procedure well and was returned to the recovery room in good condition.

Sponge count: Correct.

Estimated blood loss: Approximately 500 cc.

_____

Ima Cutter, M.D.
Surgeon

JOHN DOE, M.D.   SMITH, HARRIET #123456-7
D&T: 10/04/XX | 10/05/XX | IC/mt
Dictated by: Ima Cutter, M.D.

OPERATIVE REPORT

FIGURE 13 Radiology Report

MERCY MEDICAL CENTER
300 Main Street
Denver, CO 80201

Radiology #: 23445

PA & LATERAL CHEST   Date: 10/05/XX

The pulmonary vessels are clearly outlined and are not distended. There are not any
typical signs of redistribution. A few increased interstitial markings persist, but there
are no typical acute Kerley B-lines. There may be a little residual pleural effusion at
the costophrenic sinus and posterior gutters. Most of the pulmonary edema and effusion has
otherwise cleared. The chest is not hyperexpanded. The thoracic vertebrae show spurring
but no compression.

IMPRESSION: 1.   No signs of elevated pulmonary venous pressure or frank failure at
                     this time.
               2.   Residual pleural effusion is seen in the costophrenic sinus
                     and posterior gutters, either residual or recent congestive failure.

BILATERAL MAMMOGRAMS   Date: 10/05/XX

Bilateral xeromammograms were obtained in both the mediolateral and craniocaudal
projections. There is no previous exam for comparison. There is slight asymmetry of the
ductal tissue in the lower outer quadrant of the right breast. There are no dominant
masses, clusters of microcalcifications or pathologic skin changes identified.

IMPRESSION: Normal bilateral mammogram.

                                      _____
                                      Renny Genray, M.D.
                                      Radiologist

JOHN DOE, M.D.   SMITH, HARRIET #123456-7
D&T: 10/05/XX | 10/06/XX | RG/mt
Dictated by: Renny Genray, M.D.

RADIOLOGY REPORT

FIGURE 14   Pathology Report

MERCY MEDICAL CENTER
300 Main Street
Denver, CO 80201

TISSUE SUBMITTED: Ganglion, right wrist.

GROSS: This is a cyst 1.6 cm in diameter. On section it contains clear mucinous material. The cyst wall is 0.2 cm thick. The cyst is multiloculated.

MICROSCOPIC: Microsection shows a cystic structure lined by parallel rows of collagen. Multiple such cysts are present.

DIAGNOSIS: Ganglion, right wrist.

                                        _____
                                        Lil Culture, M.D.
                                        Pathologist

JOHN DOE, M.D.   SMITH, HARRIET #123456-7
D&T: 10/06/XX | 10/07/XX | LC/mt
Dictated by: Lil Culture, M.D.

PATHOLOGY REPORT

FIGURE 15   Discharge Summary Report

MERCY MEDICAL CENTER
300 Main Street
Denver, CO 80201

HISTORY OF PRESENT ILLNESS: The patient is a 32-year-old, white, widowed woman who came in to the Mercy Medical Center Emergency Room complaining of dyspnea. She had been having these symptoms for over one month. The patient was told in her childhood that she exhibited some asthmatic symptoms, although she had never been formally treated for same.

Past History: She had a tonsillectomy and adenoidectomy at age 12.

Social History: She is widowed; her husband died two years ago.

Family History: The patient has two brothers, ages 28 and 30; neither has had similar breathing problems. She has two children who are in high school. The patient's mother died of a myocardial infarction. The patient's father, who is living, has had carcinoma of the colon and a transurethral resection of the prostate, and he has a history of asthma.

PHYSICAL EXAMINATION: Normocephalic and atraumatic. Pupils were equal, round and reactive to light and accommodation. No icterus. No nystagmus. Funduscopic examination was negative. Right pinna: There was some minimal swelling and edema around the ear lobe; it was nontender. Nose: There was some mild rhinitis. The throat was clear. Neck: Supple and nontender. There was no adenopathy and no jugular venous distention. No nuchal rigidity. Chest: There were rales and rhonchi on expiration. Breath sounds were shallow. Abdomen: Soft and nontender. Active bowel sounds. There was no hepatosplenomegaly. Neurologic: Patellar reflexes were 2+. Deep tendon reflexes were 2+ bilaterally. No Babinskis. Normal motor and sensory exam.

LABORATORY DATA: A CBC showed a white count of 19,000 with a left shift, a hemoglobin of 13.4 grams percent, a hematocrit of 48 volumes percent, and platelet count of 100,000. The differential showed 3 bands, 5 lymphs, 7 monos and 3 eosinophils.

HOSPITAL COURSE: The patient was admitted to the 2-North Unit. A consultation was made by Dr. Gloria B. Lopez of the pulmonology department. The differential diagnoses included the diagnosis of rule out pulmonary embolus.

CONTINUED

JOHN DOE, M.D.   SMITH, HARRIET #123456-7
D&T: 10/15/XX | 10/16/XX | JD/mt

DISCHARGE SUMMARY

FIGURE 15 (Continued): Discharge Summary Report

Page 2

The following day a pulmonary angiogram was done and placement of a Swan-Ganz catheter was done. The patient tolerated the procedure well.

The patient was placed on a heparin drip. She showed rapid improvement. Pro times and partial thromboplastin times were recorded every other day. A PA and lateral chest x-ray was done, and it showed improvement from previous studies. Intakes and outputs were constantly monitored, and a Foley catheter, which had been placed prior to surgery, was maintained for three days. The patient began taking a soft diet on the third postoperative day, and by the fifth postoperative day she was back on a normal diet.

Coincidentally, a ganglion cyst was diagnosed and removed from the patient's right wrist.

The patient made a rapid recovery and was discharged on the eleventh postoperative day. She was ambulating well and her breathing was quite improved from its status on admission.

CONDITION ON DISCHARGE: Improved.

FOLLOW-UP: The patient is to follow up with Dr. Gloria B. Lopez two days after discharge.

DISCHARGE MEDICATIONS: Coumadin #50, 10 mg p.o. q.d., Tylenol regular strength p.r.n. pain, Azmacort inhaler, and Benadryl Hcl 25 mg t.i.d. p.r.n.

DISCHARGE DIAGNOSES:
1. Asthma.
2. Pulmonary embolus, resolved.
3. Ganglion cyst, right wrist.

John Doe, M.D.
Attending Physician

JOHN DOE, M.D.   SMITH, HARRIET #123456-7
D&T: 10/15/XX | 10/16/XX | JD/mt

DISCHARGE SUMMARY

Unit 5

Medical Office Charting and Correspondence

Overview: Medical office records differ greatly from hospital medical reports. While there are six major types of reports used in hospitals, medical offices usually use only two types of medical records: the chart note and the letter. Whether a medical transcriptionist plans to work in a hospital, a clinic, a medical office, a medical transcription service, or another setting, he or she will likely at some point encounter medical office charting and should be acquainted with the procedures and formats of same.

5-A   The Role of Medical Office Charting

You have discovered that medical offices operate differently from hospitals in terms of medical transcription and medical records. In hospitals, patients usually are admitted for a short period of time or are seen, receive short-term treatment and are referred elsewhere. Each new hospital admission is treated separately and a new set of reports is made for each admission.

In medical offices, however, patients are usually seen at more frequent intervals. The evaluation and treatment for each visit may be separate or linked to a previous or future visit, and the patient records in the medical office reflect this continuity. Notes from one visit may be added to a previous record, or all records may be combined.

In medical offices, the turnaround time is usually more rigid than in a hospital. Although legally the requirements for turnaround time are 72 hours or less for a physician's office, since medical office patients are seen at more frequent intervals than in hospitals, the physician usually requests a turnaround time of 24 hours or less so that if the patient comes in for re-evaluation all the patient's records will be posted in the chart.

5-B   Types of Chart Notes

There are generally three instances in which patients would present themselves or be referred to a physician's office, and three corresponding types of chart notes: the work-up, the check-up and the follow-up.

The Work-Up. When seeing a physician for the first time, a patient usually comes, or presents, for a work-up. At this type of visit the physician investigates, or works up the patient's problem or complaints. The work-up is made on three levels: the symptoms (the patient's perceived, or subjective, complaints), the signs (the physician's observable and verifiable, or objective, findings), and the diagnosis (the analysis of the patient's condition). When dictating the work-up, the physician will usually narrate the patient's history (which would include the symptoms), a physical examination (which would include the signs of the problem), an assessment (the diagnosis) and a plan (the long-term goals and direction of the treatment).

The Check-Up. You are probably aware that yearly physical examinations, or check-ups, are recommended by physicians to their patients as a way of maintaining good health. Also, frequent check-ups on newborns and the elderly are necessary to check growth and progress or deterioration. A check-up is not performed on a new patient, but on a patient who has been seen by the physician before. When dictating the check-up, the physician usually focuses on the physical findings, since the history already is usually known and has been explored. There is usually an assessment, and a plan and brief mention of the history may be made.

The Follow-Up. After the initial evaluation and treatment of a patient's problem, he or she is often scheduled to come back to the physician's office for a recheck, or a follow-up visit. At this visit the physician re-evaluates and re-examines the patient. Since the follow-up is tied to a previous report, either a work-up or a check-up, when dictating this report the physician generally focuses on the assessment and plan. The physician usually also recommends a new follow-up date in this report. There may be a brief physical exam included in the report, or a mention of changes in the patient's problem, and some reference to the history may be made.

5-C   Types of Medical Office Correspondence

Medical office correspondence consists of letters dictated by the physician. There are two basic categories of physicians in private practice, the internist and the specialist, and their correspondence varies accordingly. Internists dictate primarily letters that introduce a patient or letters of follow-up, while the majority of the specialist's correspondence is based on work-up or follow-up of a referred patient. Physicians also dictate letters going to insurance companies, medical review boards, other physicians, and personal correspondence.

5-D   Formats for Chart Notes and Correspondence

The following tips on chart notes should be observed:

1. Chart notes are usually dictated in either the SOAP or the HPIP format.

    The SOAP format is as follows:

    S — SUBJECTIVE (History, or what the patient tells the physician)

    O — OBJECTIVE (Physical examination, or what the physician finds on exam)

    A — ASSESSMENT (The physician's impression of the problem or the diagnosis)

    P — PLAN (What the planned course of treatment for the patient will be)

    The HPIP format is as follows:

    H — HISTORY (equivalent to Subjective)

    P — PHYSICAL EXAMINATION (equivalent to Objective)

    I — IMPRESSION (equivalent to Assessment)

    P — PLAN (equivalent to Plan)

2. Often times, parts of the SOAP report and the HPIP report are interchanged. Transcribe what the physician dictates, so if a history followed by an objective section is dictated, transcribe the report as such.

3. A third type of chart note format is the problem-oriented format. This format begins with the first problem the patient complains of, and a subjective, objective, assessment and plan of that problem, and then goes on to the next problem. This problem-oriented format is often used for check-ups.

    The following tips should be observed on medical office correspondence:

1. There are three basic types of letter styles used in medical office correspondence: the full block style, the modified block style and the modified semi-block style. However, physicians may work with the medical transcriptionist to develop an individual style that may be a combination or variation of these three styles.

2. Always ask whether a physician prefers letters to be left justified (with the text lining up on the left margin) or fully justified (with the text equally spaced between and lining up on both the left and right margins).

3. Always ask whether a physician prefers open punctuation (no punctuation after salutations and complimentary closes) or mixed punctuation (the salutation is punctuated with a colon and the complimentary close is punctuated with a comma). Most physicians tend to prefer mixed punctuation, but this may vary from dictator to dictator.

4.   Ask how the physician prefers to have the dateline, the reference line, special mailing notations, attention lines and subject lines typed.

5.   Many clinics and offices are now using the notation of pc: (photocopy) instead of cc: (carbon copy) to indicate that a copy needs to be sent, since the photocopier has replaced carbon paper in most facilities. Consult the facility's procedures manual for preferences.

6.   The last word on a page should not be divided.

7.   Try to avoid "widows" and "orphans" in a letter. A widow is one line of text at the top of a page separated from the rest of the paragraph of which it is a part; the remainder of the paragraph is located on the previous page. An orphan is one line of text at the bottom of a page separated from the rest of the paragraph of which it is a part; the remainder of the paragraph is located on the next page.

8.   If a letter is too short to divide the last paragraph correctly, you can condense and complete the letter on the first page by removing spaces before and/or after the dateline, putting suite numbers on the same line as the street address, and making copy and enclosure notations single-spaced instead of double-spaced.

9.   The complimentary close and the signature block should not stand alone on a page. Make a page break in a position that provides at least two lines of text preceding the complimentary close on the page containing the complimentary close and signature block.

The SOAP format for a chart note is shown in Figure 16. Figure 17 demonstrates the problem-oriented format for a chart note. Figures 18, 19 and 20 demonstrate different types of letter styles.

FIGURE 16 Chart Note, SOAP Format

PATIENT NAME: Mary Jones
DATE: January 21, 19XX

SUBJECTIVE: This is a teenager who has had a long history of recurring tonsillitis.
Apparently last year she was not having too many problems, but she did as a younger child.
They moved here last year, and she has been having essentially monthly episodes of
tonsillitis, with a sore throat, fever, and some toxicity that usually responds to
penicillin quite quickly. She is a nonsnorer and has been having problems eating solids.

OBJECTIVE: There is a 4+ right tonsil, with some deep crypts and debris. The left side is
3+ and similarly affected. There are shotty cervical nodes anteriorly. The remainder is
unremarkable.

ASSESSMENT: Recurring and chronic tonsillitis, with marked hypertrophy and cryptic changes.

PLAN: We discussed the pros and cons of tonsillectomy, which I recommend to them. I let
them know about the specific risks involved. Since it looks like she is acutely infected
currently, I put her on amoxicillin 250 t.i.d. for 10 days. The parents will give it some
thought and call back if they want to schedule it. I told them that we should put her on
antibiotics a week ahead of time to try to prevent an acute flare-up.

MD/mt

FIGURE 17 Chart Note, Problem-Oreiented Format

PATIENT NAME: Mary Jones
DATE: January 21, 19XX

Problem 1) Tonsillitis.

SUBJECTIVE: This is a youngster who has had a long history of recurring tonsillitis.
Apparently last year she was not having too many problems, but she did as a younger child.
They moved here last year, and she has been having essentially monthly episodes of
tonsillitis, with a sore throat, fever, and some toxicity that usually responds to penicillin
quite quickly. She is a nonsnorer and has been having problems eating solids.

   OBJECTIVE: There is a 4+ right tonsil, with some deep crypts and debris.
   The left side is 3+ and similarly affected. There are shotty cervical
   nodes anteriorly. The remainder is unremarkable.

   ASSESSMENT: Recurring and chronic tonsillitis, with marked
   hypertrophy and cryptic changes.

      PLAN: We discussed the pros and cons of tonsillectomy,
      which I recommend to them. I let them know about the
      specific risks involved. Since it looks like she is
      acutely infected currently, I put her on amoxicillin
      250 t.i.d. for 10 days. The parents will give it some
      thought and call back if they want to schedule it. I
      told them that we should put her on antibiotics a week
      ahead of time to try to prevent an acute flare-up.

P 2) Right ear pain.

   S: The child has been complaining of right ear pain and pressure for about a week. She has
   had no drainage from the ear, but the mother has noticed some possible decrease in her
   hearing, as she constantly asks for the television to be turned up when others are comfortable
   with its sound. She has a previous history of a possible left otitis media, but she has never
   been evaluated for tubes.

   O: In the right ear the tympanic membrane is dull, beefy red and
   retracted. The left ear is normal. Audiogram done today shows some mild
   right-sided high-frequency hearing loss. The tympanogram in the right
   ear is type B.

      A: Otitis media, right ear.

         P: Augmentin 250 mg t.i.d. for two weeks. Tylenol for
         pain. Recheck after the medication has been completed.
         Consider possible consultation with an
         otolaryngologist for tube evaluation.

JD/mt

FIGURE 18   The Full Block Letter Style

ASSOCIATES OF OTOLARYNGOLOGY
300 Main Street
Suite 200
Aurora, Colorado 80011

Jason Jones, M.D.   Samuel Smythe, M.D.

January 1, 19XX

John Smith, M.D.
Colorado General Practitioners, P.C.
12345 Broadway
Denver, CO 80201

via REGISTERED MAIL

RE: Mrs. Mary Jones

Dear Dr. Smith:

Thank you for referring Mrs. Jones. She is a 51-year-old woman who notes several symptoms for the past three months. She has noticed a left neck lump that has gotten slightly bigger and more tender over this period of time. She says it seemed to improve a bit while she was on Keflex, but then it came back when she stopped it. She also complains of some chronic hoarseness and cough. There has also been a lot of pressure-type headache, nasal congestion and thick, yellowish discharge. She smokes one pack per day, but was a heavier smoker earlier. She says she only drinks a few beers per week. She has also had some fever off and on. She says that she had a diagnosis of vocal cord polyps at one time several years ago.

The exam revealed a hoarse woman who was slightly nervous and just slightly above desirable weight. The tympanic membranes were clear. The audiogram and tympanogram were normal. The nasal exam shows a mild left septal deviation, with quite severe rhinitis and a lot of yellow exudate. The sinuses are nontender. The oropharynx reveals a lot of thick, yellow post-nasal drip. The neck exam revealed a 1 x 1.5 cm, soft, tender mass over the left anterior cervical region, with quite prominent pulsations presumably transmitted from the deeper carotid.

Letter to Dr. John Smith
RE: Mrs. Mary Jones
January 1, 19XX
Page 2

She has several symptoms that could be ominous. We went ahead with a fiberoptic exam of the larynx, and it revealed some moderate laryngitis, along with a little bit of thickening of the left anterior vocal cord with perhaps some early leukoplakia present. Our hope is that this may predominantly be from a chronic sinusitis, of which she has very strong symptoms and physical findings.

We are going to go ahead and treat her accordingly with having her finish the Keflex that she has for another four days and then start Bactrim DS b.i.d. for another 10 days. In addition, we started her on Beconase AQ, Respaire and some Florinal with codeine for the pain and headache. We warned her very strongly that she needs to come back for a recheck in two weeks, and, especially if the left neck lump has not improved, we will do a needle biopsy that day. We will continue to follow all the other problems until they resolve or we have to do further evaluation.

We will keep you informed of her progress.

Sincerely,

Samuel Smythe, M.D.

ss/mt

Enclosures: 1) Audiogram
               2) Tympanogram

pc: Jane Miller, Audiologist
           Thomas James, M.D.

FIGURE 19 The Modified Block Letter Style

ASSOCIATES OF OTOLARYNGOLOGY
300 Main Street
Suite 200
Aurora, Colorado 80011

Jason Jones, M.D.   Samuel Smythe, M.D.

                                                     January 1, 1989

John Smith, M.D.
Colorado General Practitioners, P.C.
12345 Broadway
Denver, CO 80201

via REGISTERED MAIL

        RE: Mrs. Mary Jones

Dear Dr. Smith:

Thank you for referring Mrs. Jones. She is a 51-year-old woman who notes several symptoms for the past three months. She has noticed a left neck lump that has gotten slightly bigger and more tender over this period of time. She says it seemed to improve a bit while she was on Keflex, but then it came back when she stopped it. She also complains of some chronic hoarseness and cough. There has also been a lot of pressure-type headache, nasal congestion and thick, yellowish discharge. She smokes one pack per day, but was a heavier smoker earlier. She says she only drinks a few beers per week. She has also had some fever off and on. She says that she had a diagnosis of vocal cord polyps at one time several years ago.

The exam revealed a hoarse woman who was slightly nervous and just slightly above desirable weight. The tympanic membranes were clear. The audiogram and tympanogram were normal. The nasal exam shows a mild left septal deviation, with quite severe rhinitis and a lot of yellow exudate. The sinuses are nontender. The oropharynx reveals a lot of thick, yellow post-nasal drip. The neck exam revealed a 1 x 1.5 cm, soft, tender mass over the left anterior cervical region, with quite prominent pulsations presumably transmitted from the deeper carotid.

Dr. John Smith   -2-   January 1, 19XX

She has several symptoms that could be ominous. We went ahead with a fiberoptic exam of the larynx, and it revealed some moderate laryngitis, along with a little bit of thickening of the left anterior vocal cord with perhaps some early leukoplakia present. Our hope is that this may predominantly be from a chronic sinusitis, of which she has very strong symptoms and physical findings.

We are going to go ahead and treat her accordingly with having her finish the Keflex that she has for another four days and then start Bactrim DS b.i.d. for another 10 days. In addition, we started her on Beconase AQ, Respaire and some Fiorinal with codeine for the pain and headache. We warned her very strongly that she needs to come back for a recheck in two weeks, and, especially if the left neck lump has not improved, we will do a needle biopsy that day. We will continue to follow all the other problems until they resolve or we have to do further evaluation.

We will keep you informed of her progress.

                              Sincerely,

                              Samuel Smythe, M.D.

SS/mt

Enclosures: 1)   Audiogram
              2)   Tympanogram

pc: Jane Miller, Audiologist
        Thomas James, M.D.

FIGURE 20 The Modified Semi-Block Letter Style

ASSOCIATES OF OTOLARYNGOLOGY
300 Main Street
Suite 200
Aurora, Colorado 80011

Jason Jones, M.D.   Samuel Smythe, M.D.

January 1, 19XX

John Smith, M.D.
Colorado General Practitioners, P.C.
12345 Broadway
Denver, CO 80201

via REGISTERED MAIL

            RE: Mrs. Mary Jones

Dear Dr. Smith:

    Thank you for referring Mrs. Jones. She is a 51-year-old woman who notes several
symptoms for the past three months. She has noticed a left neck lump that has gotten
slightly bigger and more tender over this period of time. She says it seemed to improve a bit while she was on Keflex, but then it came back when she stopped it. She
also complains of some chronic hoarseness and cough. There has also been a lot of pressure-type headache, nasal congestion and thick, yellowish discharge. She smokes one
pack per day, but was a heavier smoker earlier. She says she only drinks a few beers
per week. She has also had some fever off and on. She says that she had a diagnosis
of vocal cord polyps at one time several years ago.

    The exam revealed a hoarse woman who was slightly nervous and just slightly above
desirable weight. The tympanic membranes were clear. The audiogram and tympanogram
were normal. The nasal exam shows a mild left septal deviation, with quite severe rhinitis and a lot of yellow exudate. The sinuses are nontender. The oropharynx reveals
a lot of thick, yellow post-nasal drip. The neck exam revealed a 1 x 1.5 cm, soft,
tender mass over the left anterior cervical region, with quite prominent pulsations presumably transmitted from the deeper carotid.

Dr. John Smith   -2-   January 1, 19XX

    She has several symptoms that could be ominous. We went ahead with a fiberoptic
exam of the larynx, and it revealed some moderate laryngitis, along with a little bit
of thickening of the left anterior vocal cord with perhaps some early leukoplakia present. Our hope is that this may predominantly be from a chronic sinusitis, of which
she has very strong symptoms and physical findings.

    We are going to go ahead and treat her accordingly with having her finish the
Keflex that she has for another four days and then start Bactrim DS b.i.d. for another
10 days. In addition, we started her on Beconase AQ, Respaire and some Florinal with
codeine for the pain and headache. We warned her very strongly that she needs to come
back for a recheck in two weeks, and, especially if the left neck lump has not improved, we will do a needle biopsy that day. We will continue to follow all the other
problems until they resolve or we have to do further evaluation.

    We will keep you informed of her progress.

                                        Sincerely,

                                        Samuel Smythe, M.D.

SS/mt

Enclosures: 1) Audiogram
                  2) Tympanogram

pc: Jane Miller, Audiologist
           Thomas James, M.D.

    P.S.: I hope you had a great time on your vacation in California. You missed some
horrendous weather! Let's get together for lunch or dinner soon.

Part Three

Medical Transcription Mechanics

Unit 6

Word Usage

Overview: Medical transcriptionists must not only be well-skilled in spelling, punctuation and grammar, they must also be properly trained in the correct use of words for a variety of situations. A competent transcriptionist will recognize that "there" and "their" sound alike, but have different meanings, or that "pyelography" and "cystography" are synonyms. Once familiar with phonetics, etymology, acronyms, homonyms, synonyms and antonyms, you will be able to edit correctly as well as make unclear or imprecise dictation into comprehensible and accurate word processed transcription.

6-A   Phonetics

Phonetics are keys to pronunciation. They can aid you in figuring out what a dictator is saying, or give you clues to a word's spelling.

1.   **Long (Hard) Vowel Sound Phonetics.** (Bold letters denote stressed syllable(s), capitalized letters denote phonemic sound.)

Phoneme	Word Example	Pronunciation
"A" sounds:		
AY	apex	**AY**-pecks
AY	headache	hed-**AYK**
AY	emaciate	ee-**MAY**-see-AYT
"E" sounds:		
EE	emit	**EE**-mit
EE	peroneal	pehr-oh-**NEE**-al
EE	treponeme	**chrep**-oh-NEEM
"I" sounds:		
IGH	item	**IGH**-tehm

IGH	impetigo	ehm-peh-**TIGH**-goh
IGH	benign	beh-**NIGHN**

"O" sounds:

OH	ovum	**OH**-vuhm
OH	canopy	**cahn**-OH-pee
OH	vertigo	**vehr**-tih-GOH

"U" sounds:

YOO	uvula	**YOO**V-yah-luh
YOO	cornua	**corn**-YOO-uh
YOO	menu	**mehn**-YOO

2.   **Short (Soft) Vowel Sound Phonetics.** (Bold letters denote stressed syllable(s), capitalized letters denote phonemic sound.)

Phoneme	Word Example	Pronunciation

"A" sounds:

AH/A	action	**ACK**-shun
AH/A	compassion	cuhm-**PAH**-shun

"E" sounds:

EH/E	estrogen	**ES**-troh-gin
EH/E	competent	**kahm**-PEH-tehnt

"I" sounds:

IHH/I	itch	**Ich**
IHH/I	minimal	**MIH**-nih-muhl

"O" sounds:

OHH/O	odd	**OHHD**
OHH/O	antibiotic	an-tee-bigh-**OHH**-tihk
OO	loose	**LOOS**
OO	igloo	**ihg**-LOO

"U" sounds:

UH/U	utter	**UH**-tehr
UH/U	uterus	yoo-tehr-US

3. **Keys to Pronunciation and Locating the Correct Spelling of Words.**

If the word begins with this sound:	Try this (these) spelling(s):
Vowels:	
AY...	a..., aa..., ae..., ai..., ao..., ei...
AH...	a..., au..., o..., oh...
EE...	e..., ea..., ee..., ei..., eo..., i..., y...
EH...	e..., oe...
IGH...	i..., y..., ia..., ie..., io..., ei..., ey..., ay...
IHH...	i..., y..., e..., ee..., hi...
OH...	o..., oa..., oh..., oi..., oo...
OHH...	o..., ou..., a..., au..., oh...
OO...	o..., oo..., u..., eu...
YOO...	u..., eu..., yu..., io...
UH...	u..., e..., ou...
Consonants:	
B...	b..., p...
hard C...(as in "cake")	c..., ch..., qu..., k..., g...
soft C...(as in "cement")	c..., s..., ps..., z...
D...	d..., t...
F...	f..., ph..., pf..., v..., p...
hard G...(as in "gamble")	g..., c..., qu...
soft G...(as in "giraffe")	g..., j..., ch...
H...	h..., wh..., i...
J...	j..., g..., ch...
K...	k..., c..., ch..., qu..., g...
L...	l...

M...	m..., mn..., n...
N...	n..., pn..., mn..., m...
P...	p..., f..., b..., v...
Q...	qu..., kw..., cu..., gu...
R...	r..., rh...
S...	s..., c..., ps..., z...
T...	t..., pt..., d...
V...	v..., f..., ph..., pf..., p...
hard W...(as in "wall")	w..., wh...
soft W...(as in "who")	wh..., h...
X...	x..., z..., cy...
Y...	y..., i...
Z...,	z..., x..., s..., c..., ps...

How to use the above keys to pronunciation:

a. Break down the word you are hearing into sounds and syllables.

b. Try looking up all possible word beginnings, middles, and endings, using the above sounds. The most common spelling for each sound is the first letter(s) written, and the last letter written is the least common spelling for the sound.

c. Example: dictated word: "SOO-doh-tehr-IHHG-ee-uhm". If you are unsure of the spelling, you would begin by looking under the possibilities for "S", which are "s...", "c...", "ps...", "z...", then combine the second sound "OO", which are "o...", "oo...", "u...", "eu...", the third sound, "D", which are "d...", "t...", etc. You would therefore begin looking under words beginning with "so", and not find any words beginning in "so" sounding like "SOO" followed by a "doh" sound. Therefore, you would next look under "soo", and would not find any words beginning in "soo" sounding like "SOO" followed by a "doh" sound. You would then look under "su", and you would find some words beginning in "su" sounding like "SOO" followed by a "doh" sound, but none of them with the additional sounds of "tehr", "IHHG", "ee", or "uhm". You would therefore next look under "seu", and follow the same process that you did with "so"; through the process described above, you would not find the correct word. You would next look under "co", "coo", "cu", "ceu", and not find the correct word. You would then look under "pso", "psoo", "psu", and finally "pseu", where you would see a word with the phonation similar to "SOO-doh-tehr-IHHG-ee-uhm", spelled "pseudopterygium."

6-B   Etymology

Etymology is the study of word origins. Etymology helps you to break down words by the meaning and origin of their parts. When medical transcriptionists use etymologic tools, they are aided by the meanings of the roots, prefixes and suffixes. Some of the common English, Greek and Latin prefixes, roots, suffixes and combining forms used in medical terminology follow:

Prefix Root Suffix Comb. Form	Meaning
a...	not or without (ex.: atypical behavior)
ab...	away from (ex.: abduct a muscle)
ac...	to or toward (ex.: accrue time)
acet...	vinegar (ex.: acetic acid)
acid...	sour (ex.: acidulous manner)
acou...	hearing (ex.: acoustic qualities)
act...	do, drive, or act (ex.: active)
actin...	ray or radius (ex: actinometer)
...acu...	hearing (ex.: diplacusis)
ad...	to or toward (ex.: adduct a muscle)
aden...	gland (ex.: adenoid)
adip...	fat (ex.: adipose tissue)
aer...	air (ex.: aerosol spray)
...agogue	leading or inducing (ex.: pedagogue)
...agra	catching or seizure (ex.: pellagra)
alb...	white (ex.: albino)
...alg...	pain (ex.: analgesic)
all...	other, different or atypical (ex.: allergen)
alve...	trough, channel or cavity (ex.: alveolus)
...ambu...	to move about (ex.: ambulate)

amphi...	on both sides or of both kinds (ex.: amphibian)
amyl...	starch (ex.: amylase)
an...	not or without (ex.: anaerobic)
...andr...	man (ex.: androgynous)
angi...	blood vessel (ex.: angiogram)
ankylo...	crooked or looped (ex.: ankylosis)
...ant	perform (ex.: inhalant)
ante...	before (ex.: antepartum)
anti...	against (ex.: antihistamine)
antr...	cave or cavernous (ex.: antrum of the nose)
ap...	to or toward (ex.: apprehend)
...aph...	touch (ex.: dysaphia)
apo...	away from or detached (ex.: apologetic)
aqu...	water (ex.: aqueous solution)
...ar	related to, being or resembling (ex.: molecular)
...arch...	ruler, primary, old or origin (ex.: archetype)
...arian	believer or advocate (ex.: disciplinarian)
...arter(i)...	relating to artery or main branch (ex.: arteriosclerosis)
...arthr...	joint (ex.: arthritic)
...articul...	joint (ex.: an articulated bus)
as...	to or toward (ex.: ascend)
...ase	relating to enzyme (ex.: lipase)
astr...	starlike (ex.: astrocyte)
at...	to or toward (ex.: attachment)
...ate	specific chemical compound, one acted upon, cause to become or rank (ex.: distillate or sulfate)
...athon	contest of endurance (ex.: marathon)
...ation	action or process (ex.: cremation)
...ative	related to or connected with (ex.: authoritative)
audio...	hearing or sound (ex.: audiometer)
aur...	relating to the ear (ex.: auricle)

aut...	self or automatic (ex.: autoimmune)
...bacill...	small staff or rod (ex.: diplobacilli)
...bacter...	small staff or rod (ex.: bacteriophage)
bar...	weight or pressure (ex.: barometric)
bi...	two (ex.: biannual)
bil...	relating to bile (ex.: biliary tube)
bio...	life (ex.: biochemistry)
blephar...	eyelid or cilium (ex.: blepharoplasty)
...bol...	ball (ex.: bolus)
brachi...	arm (ex.: brachium)
brachy...	short (ex.: brachycephalic)
brady...	slow (ex.: bradyarrhythmia)
bronch...	windpipe (ex.: bronchitis)
bucc...	cheek (ex.: buccal mucosa)
cac...	bad (ex.: cachexia)
...caine	synthetic anesthetic (ex.: cocaine)
calc...	stone, lime, heel (ex.: calcaneus or calculus)
calor...	heat (ex.: calorie or calorimeter)
...capit...	head or large (ex.: capitalization)
caps...	container (ex.: capsule)
carb(on)...	carbon or charcoal (ex.: carbohydrate)
carcin...	crab, cancer or tumor (ex.: carcinogen)
...cardi...	heart (ex.: cardiogram)
...cardia	heart action (ex.: tachycardia)
...carp...	wrist (ex.: carpal tunnel syndrome)
cat(a)...	down, negative (ex.: cataract)
caud...	tail (ex.: the caudal end of the parotid gland)
...cav...	hollow (ex.: concavity)
...cele	hernia (ex.: varicocele)
...cent...	hundred (ex.: century)

...cente...	puncture (ex.: amniocentesis)
...centr...	central part (ex.: centrifugal force)
...cephal...	head (ex.: encephalopathy)
cer...	wax (ex.: cerumen)
cerebr...	brain (ex.: cerebral palsy)
cervic...	neck or constricted part of an organ (ex.: cervical collar)
chancr...	cancer or ulceration (ex.: chancre sore)
cheil...	lip (ex.: cheilosis)
chem...	chemical (ex.: chemotherapy)
chir...	hand (ex.: chiropractic)
chlor...	green or greenish-yellow (ex.: chlorophyll)
chol...	bile or gall (ex.: cholelithiasis)
...chondr...	cartilage (ex.: chondroma)
chord...	string or cord (ex.: chordate)
...chori...	protective fetal membrane (ex.: chorionic)
chrom...	colored or relating to chromatin (ex.: chromosome)
chron...	time (ex.: chronological order)
...chy...	fluid or pour (ex.: ecchymosis)
...cid...	kill (ex.: insecticide)
cili...	eyelid (ex.: ciliary body)
cine...	motion picture (ex.: cineangiography)
...cipient	one who receives (ex.: recipient)
circum...	around (ex.: circumference)
...cis...	cut or kill (ex.: incisor)
...clus...	shut (ex.: occlusion)
co...	with or together (ex.: cohabitate)
...coel(e)	hollow (ex.: blastocoel)
colon...	relating to the lower intestine (ex.: colonoscopy)
colp...	hollow or vagina (ex.: colporrhaphy)
com...	with or together (ex.: communal)

con...   with or together (ex.: contraction)

corp(or)...   body (ex.: corpuscle or corpse)

crani...   skull (ex.: craniotomy)

cru...   shin or leg (ex.: cruciate)

cry...   cold (ex.: cryogenesis)

crypt...   hidden, concealed or buried (ex.: cryptograph)

cult...   tend or cultivate (ex.: culture media)

cut...   skin (ex.: cutaneous)

cyan...   blue (ex.: cyanosis)

cycl...   circle or cycle (ex.: cyclohexane)

cyst...   bladder (ex.: cystitis)

cyt...   cell (ex.: cytology)

dacry...   liquid tear (ex.: dacryon)

...dactyl...   finger, toe or digit (ex.: dactylitis)

de...   reverse, down from or reduce (ex.: decompose)

...dec(a)...   ten (ex.: decade)

...dent...   tooth (ex.: dentist)

derm(at)...   skin (ex.: dermatology)

...dextr...   right or toward the right (ex.: ambidextrous)

di...   double, through or apart, or not (ex.: diaphysis or diagonal)

dia...   through, apart or across (ex.: diameter)

...didym...   twin (ex.: epididymis)

digit...   finger or toe (ex.: digitalize)

dipl...   double (ex.: diplacusis)

dis...   opposite, not, apart, away from or exclude (ex.: disjointed)

disc...   relating to disk (ex.: discus)

dors...   back (ex.: dorsolithotomy)

...drom...   running or course (ex.: palindromia)

duct...   lead or conduct (ex.: ductitis)

duode...   twelve or relating to duodenum (ex.: duodecimal or duodenal ulcer)

dur...	hard or to last (ex.: duration)
dynam...	power (ex.: dynamite)
dys...	bad, painful or difficult, or opposite of (ex.: dysfunction)
e...	not, missing, away from or out from (ex.: edentulous)
ec...	out of (ex.: eccentric)
ecto...	outside (ex.: ectoplasmic)
ede...	swell (ex.: edema)
electro...	electrical (ex.: electron)
end...	inside (ex.: endarteritis)
...enter...	intestine (ex.: dysenteric)
epi...	upon, after or in addition (ex.: epicondylar)
erg...	work or energy (ex.: ergonomics)
erythr...	red (ex.: erythrocyte)
...esthe...	perceive or feel (ex.: anesthesia)
eu...	good, normal or wellness (ex.: euphoric)
cx...	out of, and the end of, not or former (ex.: extremity)
exo...	outside (ex.: exoskeleton)
extra...	outside of or beyond (ex.: extrapyramidal)
faci...	face (ex.: facies)
fasci...	band (ex.: fascial)
febr...	fever (ex.: febrile)
...fect...	make (ex.: effected)
ferr...	iron (ex.: ferrous oxide)
fibr...	fiber (ex.: fibrin)
fil...	thread (ex.: filament)
fiss...	split (ex.: nuclear fission)
flagell...	whip (ex.: flagellum)
...flav...	yellow (ex.: riboflavin)
...flect...	bend (ex.: inflection)
...flex...	bend (ex.: reflexion)

flu...	flow (ex.: fluid)
...for...	opening or door (ex.: perforate)
...form	shape (ex.: cuneiform)
...fract...	break (ex.: fracture)
...front...	forehead or front (ex.: bifrontal headache)
...fuge...	drive away or flee (ex.: centrifugal force)
...funct...	perform, serve or function (ex.: dysfunction)
...fus...	pour (ex.: diffusion)
galact...	milk (ex.: galactopoiesis)
gam...	marriage (ex.: gamete)
gangli...	swelling or plexus (ex.: ganglion cyst)
gastr...	stomach (ex.: gastric acid)
gelat...	freeze, congeal or gel (ex.: gelatinous fluid)
...gemin...	twin or double (ex.: bigeminy)
...gen...	become, be produced or originate (ex.: genesis)
...geo...	earth, ground or soil (ex.: geology)
...gest...	bear or carry (ex.: gestational period)
...gloss...	tongue (ex.: glossitis)
...glott...	tongue or language (ex.: epiglottis)
gluc...	sweet or sugar (ex.: glucose)
...glutin...	glue (ex.: agglutinin)
...gly...	sweet or sugar (ex.: triglyceride)
...gnath...	jaw (ex.: retrognathic)
...gno...	to know or recognize (ex.: diagnosis)
grad...	step or degree (ex.: gradient)
...gram	write or record (ex.: electrocardiogram)
gran...	grain or particle (ex.: granuloma)
...graph...	write or record (ex.: cardiographically)
...grav...	heavy or pregnant (ex.: multigravida)
gyn(ec)...	woman or female (ex.: gynecologist)

gyr...	ring or circle (ex.: gyroscope)
hect...	hundred (ex.: hectometer)
hem(at)...	blood (ex.: hematology)
hemi...	half (ex.: hemiplagia)
hepat...	liver (ex.: hepatitis)
hept...	seven (ex.: heptagon)
hered...	heir (ex.: heredity)
hex...	six (ex.: hexagon)
hist...	wet or tissue (ex.: histology)
hom...	common or same (ex.: homogenous)
...hyd(r)...	water or wet (ex.: anhydrous)
hyper...	above, beyond or extreme (ex.: hypertension)
hypn...	sleep (ex.: hypnosis)
hypo...	under, below or less than normal (ex.: hypodermic)
hyster...	womb or hysteria (ex.: hysterectomize)
...iatr...	medical or physician (ex.: podiatrist or iatrogenic)
il...	not (ex.: illiterate)
...ile...	relating to the ileum or ileus (ex.: ileostomy)
...ili...	relating to the ilium (ex.: sacroiliac)
im...	not (ex.: imperfect)
in...	not, in or on (ex.: indifferent or innate)
infra...	beneath (ex.: infraorbital)
insul...	island or isolate (ex.: insulin)
inter...	between (ex.: interstate)
intra...	within (ex.: intraocular)
ir...	not, in or on (ex.: irradiate)
irid...	rainbow or multicolored (ex.: iridescent)
ischi...	hip or hunch (ex.: ischial)
...jac...	throw (ex.: ejaculation)
...ject...	throw (ex.: ejection)

...jejun...   hungry or not partaking of food (ex.: jejunostomy)

...jug...   yoke or join (ex.: conjugate)

...junct...   yoke or join (ex.: conjunction)

...kary...   nut, kernel or nucleus (ex.: megakaryocyte)

kerat...   horn (ex.: keratin)

kil...   thousand (ex.: kilogram)

labi...   lip (ex.: labial)

lact...   milk (ex.: lactate)

lapar...   flank (ex.: laparoscopy)

laryng...   windpipe (ex.: laryngitis)

...lat...   bear or carry (ex.: elation)

...later...   side (ex.: bilateral)

...lep...   take or seize (ex.: epilepsy)

leuk...   white (ex.: leukocytosis)

...lig...   bind or tie (ex.: ligament)

lingu...   tongue or speech (ex.: linguistics)

lip...   fat (ex.: lipids)

...lith...   stone (ex.: cholelithiasis)

loc...   place (ex.: locomotion)

...log...   speak, thought or discourse (ex.: dialogue)

logy...   study of (ex.: biology)

lumb...   loin (ex.: lumbosacral spine)

...ly...   loose or dissolve (ex.: catalytic reaction)

lymph...   water or white cell containing plasma (ex.: lymphatic system)

...lysis   breaking down or decomposition (ex.: electrolysis)

macr...   long or large (ex.: macrophage)

mal...   bad or abnormal (ex.: malnutrition)

malac...   soft (ex.: chondromalacia)

mamm...   breast (ex.: mammary glands)

...man...   hand (ex.: bimanual examination)

mandib(l)...chin (ex.: mandibular)

...mani...   mental abnormality (ex.: kleptomania)

...mast...   breast (ex.: gynecomastia)

medi...   middle or median (ex.: mediastinum)

mega...   great, large or multiple (ex.: megaphone)

megal...   great or large (ex.: cardiomegaly)

melan...   black (ex.: melanoma)

...men...   month (ex.: dysmenorrhea)

...mening...   membrane, especially of the brain and spinal cord
                (ex.: meningeal)

...ment...   mind (ex.: dementia)

...mer...   part (ex.: polymer)

mes...   middle (ex.: mesoappendix)

meta...   after, beyond or accompanying (ex.: metatarsal)

metr...   measure or womb (ex.: pelvimetry or endometriosis)

micr...   short or small (ex.: microscopic)

milli...   thousand or thousandth (ex. millimeter)

...miss...   send (ex.: remission)

...mittent   send (ex.: intermittent)

...mne...   memory or remember (ex.: amnesia)

mon...   only or sole (ex.: monologue)

morph...   shape or form (ex.: morphogenesis)

...mot...   move (ex.: vasomotor)

...my...   muscle (ex.: myasthenia gravis)

...myc(es)...fungus (ex.: streptomycin)

myelo...   marrow (ex.: myelography)

myx...   mucus (ex.: myxedema)

...narc...   numbness or lethargy (ex.: narcolepsy)

nas...   nose (ex.: nasopharyngeal)

ne...   young or new (ex.: neonatal)

necr...   corpse (ex.: necrosis)

...nephr...   kidney (ex.: pyelonephritis)

neur...   nerve (ex.: neurologic)

nod...   knot (ex.: nodule)

nom...   law (ex.: astronomy)

non...   nine (ex.: nonagon)

...nos...   disease (ex.: diagnostic)

nutri...   nourish (ex.: nutrition)

ob...   against, toward or inverse (ex. obnoxious)

oc...   against, toward or inverse (ex.: occlusion)

...ocul...   eye (ex.: intraocular)

...odont...   tooth (ex.: orthodontist)

...odyn...   pain or distress (ex.: gastrodynia)

...oid   form, shape (ex.: ovoid)

...ol...   oil (ex.: cholesterolemia)

olig...   few or small (ex.: oligodontia)

oo...   egg (ex.: oophorectomy)

op...   see (ex.: hemoptysis)

ophthalm...   eye or vision (ex.: ophthalmoscope)

or...   mouth (ex.: oral)

...orb...   circle (ex.: periorbital)

orchi...   testicle (ex.: orchitis)

organ...   implement, instrument or organ (ex.: organism)

orth...   straight, right, correct or normal (ex.: orthopnea)

oss...   bone (ex.: ossify)

ost(e)...   bone (ex.: osteopathy)

ot...   ear (ex.: otology)

...ov...   egg (ex.: synovium)

oxy...   sharp or relating to oxygen (ex.: paroxysmal)

pachy(n)...   thicken (ex.: pachyderm)

par...   to give birth (ex.: multiparous)

para...	beside or beyond (ex.: parameter)
part...	bear or give birth (ex.: postpartum)
path...	disease or sickness (ex.: pathogen)
ped...	foot or child (ex.: pedal edema or pediatrician)
...pel	drive or send forth (ex.: compel)
pell...	skin or hide (ex.: pellagra)
...pellent	drive or send forth (ex.: repellent)
...pen...	need or lack of (ex.: erythrocytopenia)
...pend...	hanging down (ex.: appendix)
pent(a)...	five (ex.: pentameter)
...pep(s)...	digest (ex.: dyspepsia)
per...	through (ex.: perambulate)
peri...	around (ex.: perimeter)
...pha(s)...	speak (ex.: dysphasia)
phac...	lentil or lens (ex.: phacotoxic)
phag...	eat (ex.: phagocytosis)
pharmac...	drug (ex.: pharmacology)
pharyng...	throat (ex.: pharyngitis)
...pher...	bear or support (ex.: periphery)
...phil...	to like or have an affinity for (ex.: hydrophilic)
phleb...	vein (ex.: phlebolith)
phleg...	burn or inflame (ex.: phlegmatic)
phob...	fear (ex.: acrophobia)
phon...	sound (ex.: phonation)
phot...	light (ex.: photophobia)
...phrag...	fence or wall (ex.: diaphragmatic)
...phren...	mind or midriff (ex.: costophrenic)
...phy...	to beget or bring forth (ex.: osteophyte)
...phylac...	guard (ex.: prophylactic)
...physe...	blow or inflate (ex.: emphysema)

...pil...   hair (ex.: depilatory)

placent...   cake (ex.: placenta)

...plast...   mold or shape (ex.: angioplasty)

platy...   broad or flat (ex.: platypus)

...pleg...   strike or paralysis (ex.: paraplegic)

...plet...   fill (ex.: completion)

pleur...   rib, side or lateral (ex.: pleural effusion)

...plex...   strike or paralysis (ex.: apoplexy)

...plic...   fold (ex.: duplicate)

pne...   breathing (ex.: orthopnea)

pneum(at)...breath or air (ex.: pneumatic pressure)

pneumo(n)...lung (ex.: pneumothorax)

pod...   foot (ex.: podiatry)

pol...   pole or sphere (ex.: polar)

poly...   much or many (ex.: polymorphic)

pont...   bridge (ex.: cerebral pontine)

...posit...   put, place or position (ex.: deposit)

post...   after, behind or later than (ex.: post-traumatic)

pre...   prior to, before or in front of (ex.: preauricular)

presby...   old age (ex.: presbycusis)

pro...   earlier than, anterior or favoring (ex.: prolapse)

proct...   anus (ex.: proctology)

pseud...   false or spurious (ex.: pseudopregnancy)

psych...   soul or mind (ex.: psychosomatic)

...pto...   fall (ex.: ptosis)

pub...   adult or mature (ex.: pubescent)

pulmo(n)... lung (ex.: pulmonology)

..puls...   drive (ex.: propulsion)

punct...   pierce (ex.: puncture)

...pur...   related to pus (ex.: suppurative otitis media)

pyo...	related to pus (ex.: pyorrhea)
pyel...	trough, basin or pelvis (ex.: pyelography)
pyl...	door or orifice (ex.: pyloric)
pyr...	fire (ex.: pyromania)
quadr...	four (ex.: quadriceps)
quin(que)...	five (ex.: quintuplets)
radi...	ray (ex.: radius)
re...	back or again (ex.: reanastomosis)
ren...	kidneys (ex.: renogram)
retro...	backwards (ex.: in retrospect)
...rhag...	break or burst (ex.: hemorrhagic)
...rhaph...	suture (ex.: herniorrhaphy)
...rhe...	flow (ex.: diarrhea)
rhin...	nose (ex.: rhinoplasty)
rot...	wheel (ex.: rotator)
rub...	red (ex.: bilirubin)
salpin(g)...	tube or trumpet-like (ex.: salpingogram)
sanguin...	blood (ex.: serosanguineous)
sarc...	flesh (ex.: sarcoma)
scler...	hard (ex.: muscular sclerosis)
sclera...	related to the white of the eye (ex.: sclerae)
scop...	look or observe (ex.: endoscopy)
...sect...	cut (ex.: dissection)
semi...	half (ex.: semisoft)
sens...	perception or feeling (ex.: sensorium)
...sep...	rot or decay (ex.: antiseptic)
sept...	seven, or fence or wall (ex.: septum)
ser...	watery substance (ex.: serum)
sex...	six (ex.: sextet)
sial...	saliva (ex.: sialadenitis)

sin...	hollow or fold (ex.: sinus)
...sit...	foot (ex.: parasite)
...solut...	set free or dissolve (ex.: dissolution)
...solvent	something which sets free or loosens (ex.: dissolvent)
somat...	body (ex.: psychosomatic)
spas...	pull or draw (ex.: spasmodic)
spect(r)...	see or appear (ex.: spectrum)
sperm(at)...	seed (ex.: spermatozoa)
...spers...	scatter (ex.: disperse)
sphen...	wedge (ex.: sphenoid)
spher...	ball (ex.: spherical)
sphygm...	pulsation (ex.: sphygmomanometer)
spin...	spine or spindle (ex.: spinous ligaments)
...(s)pirat...	breathe (ex.: inspiratory)
splen...	spleen (ex.: splenectomy)
spor...	seed (ex.: sporogenesis)
squam...	scale or scaly (ex.: squamous)
sta...	make stand or stop (ex.: static)
stal...	send (ex.: peristalsis)
staphyl...	bunch of grapes, uvula (ex.: Staphylococcus)
stear...	fat (ex.: stearate)
ster...	solid (ex.: cholesterol)
...sthen...	strength (ex.: myasthenia)
...stol...	send (ex.: diastolic)
stom(at)...	mouth or orifice (ex.: anastomosis)
strep(h)...	twist (ex.: Streptococcus)
...strict...	draw tight, compress or cause pain (ex.: constriction)
...stringent	something that draws tight or compresses (ex.: astringent)
...stroph...	twist (ex.: catastrophic)
...struct...	pile up or mount against (ex.: obstructive)

sub...	under or below (ex.: submental)
super...	beyond or extreme (ex.: supersede)
sym...	with or together (ex.: sympathy)
syn...	with or together (ex.: synopsis)
...ta...	stretch or put under tension (ex.: atelectasis)
tachy...	fast or quickened (ex.: tachycardia)
...tact...	touch or feel (ex.: contact)
...tax...	order or arrange (ex.: ataxia)
...tect...	cover (ex.: protection)
...teg...	cover (ex.: integument)
tele...	far, at a distance (ex.: telescopic)
tempor...	time or temple (ex.: temporomandibular)
ten(d)...	stretch (ex.: tendinitis)
test...	relating to the testicle (ex.: testitis)
tetra...	four (ex.: tetrahedron)
...the...	put or place (ex.: synthetic)
therap...	treatment (ex.: therapeutic)
therm...	heat (ex.: thermodynamics)
thi...	sulfur (ex.: thioglycolate)
thorac...	chest (ex.: thoracolumbar)
thromb...	lump or clot (ex.: thrombocytopenia)
...thym...	spirit (ex.: dysthymic)
thyr...	shield (ex.: thyroid)
...toc...	childbirth (ex.: dystocia)
...tom...	cut (ex.: craniotomy)
...ton...	stretch (ex.: peritoneal)
top...	place (ex.: topical anesthesia)
tors...	twist (ex.: torsion)
tox...	poison (ex.: toxic)
trache...	windpipe (ex.: tracheostomy)

...tract...   draw or drag (ex.: contraction)

trans...   across, so as to change (ex.: transcend or transcription)

trauma(t)...   wound (ex.: traumatic)

tri...   three (ex.: triangle)

trich...   hair (ex.: trichoid)

trip...   rub (ex.: lithotripsy)

trop...   turn, change or react (ex.: tropical)

troph...   nutritive (ex.: atrophy)

tuber...   swelling, node or resembling a tube (ex.: tuberculosis)

typ...   type (ex.: atypia)

typh...   fog or stupor (ex.: typhoid)

un...   one or not (ex.: unilateral or unrelated)

ur...   related to urine (ex.: dysuria)

vacc...   cow (ex.: vaccination)

vagin...   sheath or related to the vagina (ex.: invagination)

vas...   vessel (ex.: vasculature)

...ver(t)...   turn (ex.: divert)

vesic...   bladder or sac (ex.: vesicle)

vit...   life (ex.: revitalize)

...vuls...   pull or twitch (ex.: convulsion)

xanth...   yellow or blond (ex.: xanthic acid)

...yl...   substance (ex.: pterodactyl)

zo...   life (ex.: zoology)

zyg...   yoke or union (ex.: zygote)

zym...   ferment (ex.: enzyme)

6-C   Acronyms

Acronyms are words made up of the first letters of a series of words in a phrase, which are sometimes pronounced as a word. Try to use the series of words when possible instead of the acronyms, unless it is the physician's or the hospital's personal style, or a widely accepted form. Following are some common acronyms (an asterisk preceding denotes the acronym is acceptable in most transcription on first reference):

*AIDS — acquired immune deficiency syndrome

CABG — coronary artery bypass graft

ECHO — enteric cytopathic human orphan (virus)

*ECoG — electrocochleography

EOMI — extraocular movements intact

*FANA — fluorescent antinuclear antibody

*HEENT — head, ears, eyes, nose and throat

MAST — military antishock treatment

PERRLA — pupils equal, round and reactive to light and accommodation

*REM — rapid eye movement

*SIDS — sudden infant death syndrome

SOAP — subjective, objective, assessment, plan

*TENS - transcutaneous electrical nerve stimulation

Some acronyms have become so common that they are now acceptable words. When acronyms become acceptable words, they are written in lowercase. Following are some examples:

laser (light amplification by stimulated emission of radiation)

radar (radio detecting and ranging)

dopa (dihydroxyphenylalanine)

scuba (self-contained underwater breathing apparatus)

snafu (situation normal, all fouled up)

6-D   Homonyms

Homonyms are words that sound or are pronounced alike, but are different in meaning. Following are examples:

aural (pertaining to the ears) vs. **oral** (pertaining to the mouth)

coarse (thick) vs. **course** (a path or regimen)

complement (that which completes) vs. **compliment** (a praise)

ileum (intestine) vs. **ilium** (hip bone)

principal (primary) vs. **principle** (a rule or law)

their (belonging to them) vs. **there** (a place away from here)

6-E   Synonyms

Synonyms are words that have the same meaning. Some examples follow:

good = just = pure = kind = generous

difficult = complex = laborious = hard = strenuous

sound = audibility = acoustics = sonification = bruit

disease = illness = sickness = ailment = malady

6-F   Antonyms

Antonyms are words that have opposite meanings. Some examples follow:

hypertension (high blood pressure) vs. **hypotension** (low blood pressure)

principal (main) vs. **secondary** (less important)

macroscopic (visible to the naked eye) vs. **microscopic** (visible only with enlargement)

abduct (to flex away from) vs. **adduct** (to flex towards)

bradycardia (slow pulse rate) vs. **tachycardia** (fast pulse rate)

Unit 7

Sentence Grammar

Overview: A medical transcriptionist should have a thorough command of the English language. He or she must be especially proficient in grammar skills. A transcriptionist should understand in detail parts of speech and sentence structure, including nouns, verbs, adverbs, adjectives, subjects, objects, predicates, clauses, articles, conjunctions, interjections, and prepositions. An explanation of each (with examples in **bold** print) follows.

7-A   Nouns

Nouns are words that refer to persons, places, things, ideas or qualities. Nouns are used more frequently than any other part of speech, and many sentences contain more than one noun. Nouns are classified as proper, common, concrete, abstract, collective and verbal.

1. Proper nouns are formal names of persons, places and things, and are capitalized.

    Examples:

    Bob went to **Mercy Hospital.**

    I found out that **Dr. Miller** attended school in **Detroit, Michigan.**

    Chairman Roger Rose attended the **Parkinson's Disease Symposium.**

2. Common nouns are more casual names and words, and are not capitalized.

    Examples:

    The **mother** took her **child** to the **emergency room.**

    She took the **gurney** into the surgical **area.**

    The **physician** worked with the **psychologist.**

3. Concrete nouns are common nouns that refer to things we can perceive with the physical senses of sight, sound, smell, taste and touch.

73

Examples:

The physician noted the **smell** of **ethanol** on the patient's **breath**.

A purulent **drainage** was emanating from the **wound**.

She palpated a **stone** in the **gland**.

4.   Abstract nouns are words that refer to things that cannot be perceived with the physical senses, such as ideas or qualities.

Examples:

The guest speaker had an enlightened **philosophy**.

Her **theories** broke **convention**.

The surgeon proposed electrocautery as a **solution** to the **problem**.

5.   Collective nouns are words that identify groups. Although collective nouns can express more than one person or thing, they are usually regarded as singular words.

Examples:

A **committee** selects medical school candidates.

The patient had suffered a sting after being surrounded by a **swarm** of bees.

His **family** consented to the risks of the procedure.

6.   Verbal nouns are words that begin with a verb and end in "-ing", but function as nouns. Verbal nouns are also called gerunds.

Examples:

Editing is an important part of transcription.

The nursing student said that **studying** had always been difficult for him.

Cleaning and **dressing** a wound daily can inhibit contamination.

7-B   Subjects

Subjects are words, usually nouns or a group of words including nouns, that are the topic(s) of a sentence. The subject of a sentence can consist of words that name something, someplace or someone plus other words such as modifiers, conjunctions and prepositions.

Examples:

The hemostat was within the surgeon's reach.

He gave the patient an injection.

The result of lack of vitamin C can be scurvy.

7-C   Objects

Objects are words, usually nouns or a group of words including nouns, that receive the action of a verb. They are different from the subject of the sentence in that the subject performs an action while an action is performed upon or by an object. There are direct objects, which complete the meaning of the main verb of a sentence or clause, and indirect objects, which identify to or for whom the direct object is performed.

Examples:

The diagnosis was **leukemia.** (direct object)

He preferred **the well-trained nurse.** (direct object)

The technician gave the Bovie unit to **the first assistant.** (indirect object)

The residents asked **the professor** a question. (indirect object)

7-D   Pronouns

Pronouns are words that substitute for nouns and function in sentences like nouns. Pronouns can be classified as personal, demonstrative, relative, interrogative, reflexive, intensive and indefinite. Also, there are three cases of pronouns: the subjective case (where the pronoun is the subject in a sentence), the possessive case (where the pronoun shows possession or ownership) and the objective case (where the pronoun is the object in a sentence). Pronouns can be further identified as being singular or plural, and being first person, second person or third person (see charts below). It is especially important for transcriptionists to be familiar with classifications and cases of pronouns, as dictators often confuse the cases (switching the subjective with the objective case, and vice versa), do not use the correct pronoun, etc. Use the following as a guide:

1. Personal pronouns are noun substitutes that refer to a particular person or a group of people. Personal pronouns include the words **I, you, he, she, it, we, you, they,** etc. (Special note: If you are in doubt about which personal pronoun to use, always refer to the chart below. If the word the pronoun replaces is a subject, no matter where it occurs in a sentence, use a subjective pronoun. If the word the pronoun replaces is an object, no matter where it occurs in a sentence, use an objective pronoun. Physicians often use "I" where an objective pronoun (**me,** or **myself**)

should go. Also, remember this: *prepositional phrases take objective pronouns.)*

Examples:

I (subjective personal pronoun) gave **his** (possessive personal pronoun) book to **her** (objective personal pronoun).

They (subjective personal pronoun) showed **our** (possessive personal pronoun) flag to **you** (objective personal pronoun).

	Subjective	Possessive	Objective
Singular			
1st person	I	my, mine	me
2nd person	you	your, yours	you
3rd person	he, she, it	his, her(s), its	him, her, it
Plural			
1st person	we	our, ours	us
2nd person	you	your, yours	you
3rd person	they	their, theirs	them

2.   Demonstrative pronouns are noun substitutes that identify nouns and are always either subjective or objective in case. Demonstrative pronouns include the words **this, that, these** and **those.**

Examples:

This is larger than **that.**

These are more skilled in their art than **those.**

	Subjective	Objective
Singular	this/that	this/that
Plural	these/those	these/those

3.   Relative pronouns link a clause to another pronoun or a noun. Interrogative pronouns are noun substitutes that introduce questions. Relative pronouns include the words **who, which, that** and **what.** Interrogative pronouns include the words **who, whose, whom, whoever, whomever, which** and **what.**

Examples:

That was **what** I wanted. (reflexive pronouns)

Now tell me, who gave whose cassette to whom? (interrogative pronouns)

	Subjective	Possessive	Objective
Singular or Plural			
3rd person	who	whose	whom
	whoever	whose	whomever
	which, that, what	————	which, that, what

4. Reflexive pronouns are noun substitutes that show that the subject of the sentence also receives the action of the verb. Intensive pronouns are noun substitutes that stress a noun or another pronoun. (Special note: Reflexive/intensive pronouns either emphasize a noun or other pronoun or indicate that the subject of the sentence also receives the action of the main verb, so every time you include a reflexive or intensive pronoun, you should make sure there is an additional subject or pronoun in the sentence.)

Examples:

They have no one to blame but **themselves**. (reflexive)

I **myself** saw the physician question the patient. (intensive)

	Subjective	Possessive	Objective
Singular			
1st person			myself
2nd person			yourself
3rd person			herself, himself, itself
Plural			
1st person			ourselves
2nd person			yourselves
3rd person			themselves

5. Indefinite pronouns are special pronouns that do not substitute for a specific noun, but which refer to one or a group of unknown, or indefinite, nouns. Indefinite pronouns include the following words:

all	each	neither	one
any	either	nobody	some
anybody	everybody	none	somebody
anyone	everyone	no one	someone
anything	everything	nothing	something

a.   Indefinite pronouns always take singular pronouns:

Example:

Everybody likes **his** new computer equipment.

b.   Indefinite pronouns usually take a singular verb, but the indefinite pronouns "all", "any", "none" and "some" may take a plural verb. The indefinite pronouns "all", "any", "none" and "some" may be either singular or plural in their meanings, and the verb used with each depends on its meaning, singular or plural, within a particular sentence. If the indefinite pronoun has a singular meaning, it takes a singular verb (e.g., "some" is plural in *Some Like It Hot*, and "some" is singular in "some goes in this tube, and some in the other"), and vice versa.

Examples:

All patients **go** to admissions before having day surgery.

None of the insurance premium **covers** the cost of infertility tests.

7-E   Verbs

Verbs are words that express actions, happenings or states of being. Some sentences contain one word that serves as a verb, while other sentences contain more than one word that serves as a verb. Multiple word verbs contain helping verbs, or words beside the main verb that show changes in time or tense. Some groups of verbs can go together to express one action and become verb clauses.

Examples:

The operation **occurred** the day after the holiday.

The sinusitis **was camouflaged** by rhinitis. ("was" is a helping verb)

Many expert transcriptionists **aspire to become** physicians. ("aspire to become" is a verb clause)

1.   There are five major verb forms: the infinitive form, the present participle form, the past tense form, the past participle form, and the future tense form. The infinitive verb form is the plain form, or the form of the

verb you will find in the dictionary. You form the present participle form of a verb by adding "-ing" to the infinitive of the verb. The past tense form of a verb indicates the action of the verb happened in the past. The endings "-d" and "-ed" usually indicate the verb is in the past tense (see #2 below for exceptions). The past participle form is made by using the past tense form of the verb along with the helping verbs "has", "have" or "had" (see #2 below for exceptions). The future tense form of a verb indicates the action of the verb will happen at some time in the future. The helping verbs "will" or "shall" before the verb infinitive indicate the future tense.

Examples:

I **transcribe** medical records. (infinitive)

I like **transcribing** medical records. (present participle)

I **transcribed** medical records yesterday. (past tense)

I **had transcribed** 50 medical records by the end of the day. (past participle)

I **will transcribe** 50 medical records tomorrow. (future tense)

2.   There are two types of verbs: regular verbs and irregular verbs. Regular verbs, such as "stop", "live" and "collect", take standard endings when changing tense; irregular verbs, such as "begin", "build" and "come", take nonstandard endings or become different words entirely when changing tense. For regular verbs, to show a change in time to the past tense, you simply add a "d" or an "ed" ending. For irregular verbs, to show a change in time to the past (the past tense or the past participle forms of the verb) you need to make more changes than simply adding a "d" or an "ed". It is important for a medical transcriptionist to be familiar with irregular verb forms, as dictators sometimes use the wrong irregular verb or verb form.

Examples:

I **forgot** the answer. (irregular past tense)

He **had chosen** the five candidates. (irregular past participle)

You should memorize the past tenses and past participles of the following common irregular verbs:

Infinitive	Past Tense Form	Past Participle Form
become	became	become
begin	began	begun
break	broke	broken

bring	brought	brought
choose	chose	chosen
come	came	come
do	did	done
draw	drew	drawn
drink	drank	drunk
drive	drove	driven
eat	ate	eaten
find	found	found
forget	forgot	forgotten
get	got	gotten
give	gave	given
go	went	gone
hold	held	held
know	knew	known
lay	laid	laid
lead	led	led
leave	left	left
lie (to recline)	lay	lain
ring	rang	rung
rise	rose	risen
say	said	said
see	saw	seen
sing	sang	sung
sit	sat	sat
speak	spoke	spoken
spring	sprang	sprung
stand	stood	stood
steal	stole	stolen
swim	swam	swum

take	took	taken
tear	tore	torn
write	wrote	written

7-F   Predicates

Predicates are words, usually verbs or groups of words containing verbs, that describe actions, happenings or states of being.

Examples:

The patient **was examined** under anesthesia.

The symposium **featured** several expert proctologists.

Operations **take** time.

7-G   Adjectives

Adjectives are words that describe or modify nouns or pronouns. An adjective can be a single word or a word group that modifies. Note: Medical terms that are adjectives often end in **-ic, -al, -able, -ible,** or **-ian,** and compound adjectives often have a delineating word as a prefix such as **well-, post-, right-, left-, low-,** etc.

Examples:

The **leukorrheic** hemorrhage was a complication of the procedure.

The infant was **well nourished.**

Her **soft-spoken** manner was much appreciated.

7-H   Adverbs

Adverbs are words that describe or modify verbs, adjectives and other adverbs. Note: Very few medical terms are adverbs, but many terms that are usually adjectives can become adverbs with an -ly ending.

Examples:

The drug education was **insightful.**

The fluid was **surgically** suctioned.

The physician was **quite** intelligent.

7-I   **Clauses**

A clause (also called a phrase) is a group of related words containing a subject and a predicate that is not a complete sentence. Clauses are often set off from other parts of a sentence or other clauses by prepositions, conjunctions and clause introducers. A clause usually cannot stand on its own as a complete sentence because of its clause introducer.

Examples:

The surgeon **who performed the operation** was undertrained.

Although the risks were great, the surgery was necessary.

The syllabus, **which was part of the curriculum**, was lengthy.

A Special Note on Clauses. The words "that" and "which" are special clause introducers that are frequently confused. "That" always introduces restrictive clauses, clauses that are necessary to keep the meaning of the sentence intact. "Which" should be used to introduce only nonrestrictive clauses (clauses that are nonessential to preserve the meaning of the sentence, but give additional information), although in a few cases "which" could also introduce a restrictive clause. Generally, however, use "that" to introduce restrictive clauses and "which" to introduce nonrestrictive clauses. If you find these words incorrectly interchanged, you should try to correct them.

Examples:

The patient was a passenger in the automobile accident **that resulted in her paralysis**. (It is important to know that the automobile accident resulted in her paralysis.)

The patient injured her cervical spine in the accident, **which occurred two weeks ago**. (The fact that the accident occurred two weeks ago is incidental; the major focus of the sentence is that the patient injured her cervical spine in the accident.)

7-J   **Articles**

Articles are determiners that indicate a noun follows. Articles are the words "a", "an" or "the". The articles "a" and "an" are often confused; use "a" for a noun beginning in a consonant or a consonant sound and use "an" for a noun beginning in a vowel or a vowel sound. Also, use "an" with a soft "h" sound, as in the words "historical" and "histologic".

Examples:

The physician is on call.

A clamp is **a** surgical instrument.

An SRT test is **an** important part of making **an** otologic assessment.

Dr. Jonas Salk made **an** historical discovery.

7-K   Conjunctions

A conjunction links words, phrases and clauses. Coordinating conjunctions, which always connect two or more nouns, verbs, adjectives, adverbs, phrases or clauses, are: "and", "but", "or", "nor", "for", "so" and "yet".

Examples:

The midwife **or** the nurse practitioner will assist the patient.

Strep **and** Staph are two types of infectious processes.

The patient was prepped, **but** he was not intubated.

7-L   Interjections

An interjection is an expression of feeling or an expression that commands attention, either alone or as part of a sentence.

Examples:

Hey, read my lips!

Oh, what a feeling!

Darn!

7-M   Prepositions

1.   Prepositions are connecting words. They describe the relationship of something to something else. Following are some common prepositions:

about	above	across	after	against	along
among	around	as	at	before	behind
below	beneath	beside	between	beyond	by
despite	down	during	for	from	in
inside	into	like	near	next to	of
off	on	onto	out	out of	outside
over	past	round	since	through	throughout
to	toward	under	underneath	unlike	until
up	upon	with	within	without	

2. Prepositional phrases are clauses that contain prepositions. Following are examples of some prepositional phrases:

She is **in the boat.**

The book is **about nothing.**

She threw the ball **against the wall.**

3. Following are some rules for prepositions:

    a. Prepositions should come before their objects.

    b. Try not to begin a sentence with a prepositional phrase.

    c. Try not to end a sentence with a preposition.

7-N   Some Special Notes about Grammar

1. Use "were" with most statements expressing desire or beginning with "if".

    Examples:

    If I **were** a doctor, I would find a cure for many life-threatening diseases.

    I wish Dr. Jones **were** my primary care physician.

2. Recognize the passive voice; in medical transcription only change the passive voice to active voice when the person who performs the action is known and is important to the sentence, or when the sentence is awkward in the passive voice.

    Passive voice: The results of the test **were thought to be nondiagnostic by the** physician.

    Active voice: **The physician thought** the results of the test were non-diagnostic.

    Examples of when you should leave the passive voice as is:

    The operation **was performed.** (it is not important who performed the operation in this sentence)

    Under general anesthesia, **the patient was prepped and draped** in the normal sterile fashion. (it is not important who did the prepping and draping of the patient in this sentence)

    The octogenarian **was seen by the visiting nurse** when she went home. (the nurse is less important than the patient in this sentence)

3.   Be sure to always use verb forms of "lie", "lay", "sit" and "set" correctly. "Lie" and "sit" are intransitive verbs and cannot take objects. They are used to show the action of persons or other living things. "Lay" and "set" are transitive verbs, and almost always take objects. They are used to indicate that something is being done to an object.

Examples:

Pregnant patients are to **lie** down and take naps every afternoon.

You should have **laid** the reports on the radiologists' desks for signatures.

The bird always **sits** on the ledge outside the patient's room.

Next time, please try to **set** the gurney down without such force.

4.   Always make subjects and verbs agree in number.

a.   When subjects are joined by the conjunction "and," even if both are singular, use a plural verb.

Examples:

The scalpel **and** pursestring suture **rest** on the cart.

Hemostats **and** electrocautery **are** used in operations.

b.   When subjects are joined by the conjunction "or," the verb should agree with the closest subject.

Examples:

The pathologist **or the phlebotomists have called** in the report.

Neither the physician **nor I like** the way the patient was treated.

c.   When modifying words come between subjects and verbs, the verb should agree with the main subject.

Examples:

The physician, as well as his nurses and assistants, **has** volunteered for the blood drive.

The profits earned by one physician **were donated to** the orphanage.

5.   Always try to make sentences within a paragraph agree in tense and subject. For example, if the past tense is predominantly used throughout the paragraph, try not to use the present tense in a sentence in that same paragraph. Also, make sure the subject is always clear and consistent.

Examples:

a.   When this is dictated: "The exam **was** basically normal. The head, eyes, ears, nose and throat **were** negative; and the throat **shows** no exudates."

Type: "The exam **was** basically normal. The head, eyes, ears, nose and throat **were** negative; and the throat **showed** no exudates."

b.   When this is dictated: "The patient was advised to see his physician, Dr. Smith, in 10 days, as **he** would be out of town next week."

Type: "The patient was advised to see his physician, Dr. Smith, in 10 days, as **Dr. Smith** would be out of town next week."

Unit 8

Punctuation

Overview: Punctuation is marking or dividing words, groups of words or sentences with signs and symbols such as periods, commas or semicolons to mark the end of a thought. The correct use of punctuation is a crucial skill for the medical transcriptionist, as most dictators of medical records do not bother to include punctuation, or when the dictator does include it, it is oftentimes incorrect. Use the following as a guide for when and where to use punctuation marks.

8-A   Periods

Use periods in the following cases:

1. to end sentences that are statements, mild commands or indirect questions

    Examples:

    The nurse was kind.

    Follow my instructions.

    The patient wondered why he was given the medication.

2. with many abbreviations

    Examples:

    M.D.

    Ph.D.

    p.m.

3. to separate dollars and cents, and to separate whole numbers and decimal fractions

    Examples:

    The cost of the seminar was $140.50.

Her hematocrit count was 42.5 on admission.

The specimen measured 1.5 cm x 4.5 mm.

4. after Roman numerals, Arabic numerals and alphabetical letters used to enumerate items in an outline or list

Examples:

I.   Grammar

    A.   Nouns

        1.   Proper nouns

        2.   Common nouns

        3.   Concrete nouns

        4.   Abstract nouns

        5.   Collective nouns

        6.   Verbal nouns

    B.   Pronouns

    C.   Verbs

II.   Punctuation

    A.   Periods

    B.   Commas

    C.   Semi-colons

5. after each initial in a person's name

Examples:

J. Paul Getty

B. B. King

Michael J. Fox

6. after an abbreviation that is part of a company's official legal name

Examples:

General Dynamics, Inc.

John Adams & Assoc.

Dewey, Cheatam & Howe, Ltd.

8-B   Question Marks

Use question marks in the following cases:

1. after direct questions

   Examples:

   Do you know what the diagnosis was?

   "Will my condition improve?" asked the patient.

2. within parentheses to indicate doubt regarding a word or phrase

   Examples:

   The surgery was performed in 1979 (?).

   She had (?) diverticulitis.

3. after each of a series of items calling for individual answers

   Examples:

   Did you find the novel interesting? the characters believable? the plot realistic?

   The physician questioned the patient about his previous psychiatric admissions. One time? Two times? Three times? More?

8-C   Exclamation Points

Use exclamation points after emphatic statements, interjections or strong commands.

   Examples:

   Whew! That scalpel almost nicked me!

   When the physician saw the suture, he shouted, "What is this!"

   Call security!

8-D   Commas

Use commas in the following cases:

1. before a coordinating conjunction linking main clauses that contain both a subject and predicate

   Examples:

The surgeon performed the operation, and the physician performed the examination.

The scalpel was new, but the rest of the instruments had been used before.

2.   to set off most introductory elements, an element that modifies a word or words in the main clause that follows

Examples:

If he were a civilized person, the doctor would not be so difficult to work with.

Frustrated, the transcriptionist left a blank.

3.   to set off nonrestrictive elements, clauses and phrases, nonrestrictive meaning elements that give additional information about the word or words it applies to, but does not limit the word or words

Examples:

Transcriptionists, who turn dictation into written words, are skilled professionals.
(However: Transcriptionists who work hard will get raises [no commas].)

Good grammar, which is essential to proper medical record transcription, often times is not taught properly in elementary schools.

4.   to set off nonrestrictive appositives (an appositive is a noun or noun substitute that renames and could substitute for another noun immediately preceding it)

Examples:

The scalpel, a surgical cutting instrument, is usually an important part of operations.

All her daughters, Susan, Donna and Janice, signed the consent for operation.

5.   to set off parenthetical expressions

Examples:

The chairman of the board, according to the physician, should have a vote.

Nurses, for example, work in hospitals.

6. to set off **yes** and **no**, tag questions, words of direct address and mild interjections

Examples:

Yes, the physician has a point.

Old physicians sometimes think they're gods, don't they?

7. to set off absolute phrases

Examples:

Their work completed, the students went home.

Her stitches, the ends being frayed and rough, made her uncomfortable.

8. to set off phrases expressing contrast

Examples:

The report needs less opinion, more fact.

Hospitals are places for the sick, not the lonely.

9. between items in a series, between coordinate adjectives, and between more than one directly modifying adjective

Examples:

Food, rest and fluids are the best remedy for a cold.

The position requires typing, answering phones, filing, and preparing documents.

The dirty, rusty, dented scalpel made the physician wince.
(In this sentence the adjectives "dirty," "rusty" and "dented" each modify the noun "scalpel" and each could stand alone with "scalpel." The overall meaning of the sentence would not change if any one of these adjectives were removed.)

Exceptions:

There was bilateral mild red rhinitis and a thick yellow purulent discharge.

The right high-frequency sensorineural hearing loss was a result of presbycusis.
(In this sentence the adjectives "right," "high-frequency," and "sensorineural" each further modify each other, and do not directly modify the noun "loss." In other words, if any of these adjectives were removed the meaning of the sentence would change. Therefore, no commas should be used. This is likewise the case in the first sentence.)

10.   with dates, addresses, place names and long numbers

Examples:

The operation was performed on May 2, 1979.

A kilometer equals approximately 3,280 feet.

11.   with quotations

Examples:

The girl said, "My stomach hurts."

"I brought the papers," the patient stated.

12.   to prevent misreading

Examples:

When she found out, she left the hospital for good.

Employees who can, usually give some money to charity.

8-E   Colons

Use colons in the following cases:

1.   to introduce an explanatory phrase, clause, sentence or group of sentences

Examples:

Family History: Noncontributory, as the patient was adopted.

The reason for the decision is obvious: she failed to follow directions.

2.   to introduce a series of words, phrases or clauses

Examples:

Please bring the following to the meeting: a book, a pen and a pencil.

There are three major laboratory blood work tests: the complete blood count test, the arterial blood gas test, and the superior mesentery artery test.

3.   to introduce lengthy material that needs to be set off from the rest of a sentence in a manner other than quotation marks

Example:

The Nightingale Pledge begins like this: I solemnly pledge myself before God and in the presence of this assembly to pass my life in purity and to practice my profession faithfully.

4. to separate hours from minutes in the expression of standard time in numbers

    Example:

    The operation will begin at 8:00 a.m.

5. to follow a salutation in business correspondence

    Example:

    Dear Dr. Smith:

8-F   Semicolons

Use semicolons in the following cases:

1. to separate main clauses not joined by a coordinating conjunction

    Examples:

    The boy was sick; he had a fever.

    Some physicians speak clearly; others muffle their speech and are hard to understand.

2. to separate main clauses related by a conjunctive adverb (consequently, hence, however, indeed, instead, nonetheless, otherwise, still, then, therefore and thus)

    Examples:

    He was ill; therefore, he received treatment.

    She is to return for follow-up in two weeks; however, if she has any complaints before that time she is to call the office.

3. to separate main clauses if they are long and complex, or if they contain commas, even when they are joined by a coordinating conjunction

    Examples:

    He was cyanotic, pale and diaphoretic; and his wife brought him into the hospital.

The patient brought the following to the hospital: a gown; toiletries including a toothbrush and toothpaste, a comb and deodorant; and the surgery consent forms.

4.   between an independent clause and a transitional expression such as "for example", "that is", "namely", "instead" or "for instance" when the expression precedes a list or another independent clause.

Examples:

A food challenge involves removing foods from the diet that are likely to contain allergens; for example, you should refrain from eating eggs for one week, milk for one week, grains for one week, etc.

The patient described several episodes of partial regurgitation; that is, he suffered from gastric reflux.

8-G   Apostrophes

Use apostrophes in the following cases:

1.   before or after an "s" ending to indicate the possessive case for nouns and indefinite pronouns

Examples:

One must make one's own choices.

The twins' signs were consistent with their symptoms.

2.   to indicate the omission of one or more letters, numbers or words in a standard contraction

Examples:

It's time for the operation you're supposed to have.

The incision was made at the 3 o'clock position.

3.   to form the plurals of letters, numbers and words named as words

Examples:

Please do not forget to dot your i's and cross your t's when transcribing medical records.

The physician always confuses her a's and an's.

8-H   Quotation Marks

Use quotation marks in the following cases:

1.   to enclose direct quotations (use single quotation marks to enclose a quotation within a quotation)
     [Note: Place commas and periods inside quotation marks, place colons and semicolons outside quotation marks, and place other punctuation inside quotation marks only if they belong in the quotation. Also, place commas and periods outside quotation marks when used with single letters or single words.]

     Examples:

     "The insurance premium," the clerk explained, "has not been paid."

     "She told me 'my stomach hurts' after she swallowed the pill," the physician said.

     The patient complained of "cramping ".

2.   to enclose words or phrases that are slang or believed to be someone else's words

     Examples:

     The patient said that she had taken several "uppers and downers" before coming to the emergency room.

     Joseph thought he was "king" of the psychiatric unit.

     After I began my exam the patient stated that she had a "belly-ache ".

3.   around titles such as songs, short poems, articles in periodicals, short stories, essays, episodes of television and radio programs and subdivisions of books

     Examples:

     The patient often sang "London Bridge is Falling Down."

     Watch the episode "Diary of a Prostitute" on the *Oprah Winfrey Show* today.

     Please read Unit 2, "Microcomputer Tools: An Introduction to Word Processing."

8-I   Other Punctuation Marks

1.   **Dashes.** Use a dash:

a. to indicate an abrupt change in tone or thought

Example:

The decision—not an easy one to make—was final.

b. to set off parts of some sentences

Example:

Forceps, scalpels, sutures—these are some of the tools of surgery.

2. **Hyphens.** Use a hyphen:

a. to separate a word at the end of a line

Example:

Although the patient's differential diagnosis included both osteo-porosis and costochondritis, she had never previously been hospitalized.

b. between some prefix and root combinations

Example:

He had a non-English accent.

c. in some compound words

Example:

His mother-in-law lacked self-motivation.

d. to avoid ambiguity

Example:

She had a small-bowel exam. (versus: She had quite a small bowel.)

e. to indicate separation of the first and second parts of a hyphenated compound word group

Example:

She was given pre- and post-surgical instructions.

f. when it is necessary to write out compound numbers between 21 and 99

Example:

Thirty-two physicians were present at the symposium.

g. when writing out fractions, when they act as modifiers

Example:

A two-thirds majority of the pathologists voted "yea" at the meeting.

h.   to replace the word "to" when used as a range between numerals

Example:

He is to return to the clinic in 10-14 days.

3.   **Parentheses.** Use a set of parentheses:

a.   to enclose nonessential words, clauses or phrases that would not alter the meaning of a sentence. Use a single parenthesis to indicate numerical order

Examples:

Motor vehicles (cars, for example) must yield to ambulances.

The patient is discharged on these medications: 1) estrogen, 2) hydrochlorothiazide and 3) a Proventil inhaler.

b.   to enclose symbols or figures that illustrate, clarify or confirm a word or word group's meaning

Examples:

Use an asterisk (*) to indicate that there is a footnote at the bottom of the page.

The reimbursement for the insured should have been at a rate of five percent (5%) instead of two percent (2%).

4.   **Brackets.** Use brackets within quotations to indicate editorial comments or changes, or with a word or group of words within a parenthetical phrase that would otherwise be set off with parentheses.

Examples:

"The patient [previously known to be uncooperative] was inebriated," he said.

(Please make corrections [if necessary] here.)

They died with there [sic] boots on.

5.   **Ellipses.** Use an ellipsis (three spaced periods) to indicate omissions within quotations, to mark an unfinished sentence, or to separate.

Examples:

"I am nervous and cold . . . and confused," the patient stated.

A . . . 10 points

6.   **Slash (Virgule).** Use the slash between options or alternatives and to represent the word "per" in abbreviations.

Examples:

This is a pass/fail course.

The dosage is 20 mg/kg.

Unit 9

Compound Words and Hyphenation

Overview: Why is it necessary to be familiar with compound and hyphenated words? Compound words can be confusing, as they are a group of two or more words that convey a combination of ideas. Questions regarding hyphenation often arise in the transcription process, as hyphens are oftentimes used to accomplish combining compound words. But compound words are not always hyphenated; sometimes the words are joined without any punctuation marks at all. It is important for a medical transcriptionist to be able to identify a compound word and to be able to correctly use hyphenation or the lack of it as necessary, because, as with other punctuation, the dictator usually does not mention in his or her dictation when and how a compound word group should be combined.

9-A   Compound Words and Hyphens

1. Usually, hyphens are not necessary when using compound words that have become common in usage and are spelled as one word.

   Examples:

   earache

   nosebleed

   gallbladder

   antifreeze

2. Use a hyphen to avoid confusion, to avoid ambiguity or to avoid making an awkward combination of letters, especially with the prefixes **ante-, anti-, bi-, co-, contra-, counter-, de-, inter-, intra-, macro-, micro-, mid-, non-, out-, over-, post-, pre-, pro-, pseudo-, re-, semi-, sub-, super-, trans-, tri-, ultra-, un-.**

   Examples:

   re-creation (again created) vs. **recreation** (leisure activity) [hyphenation in the first case avoids confusion.]

re-enactment vs. **reenactment** [hyphenation in the first case avoids placing two identical vowels together.]

childlike vs. **pill-like** [lack of hyphenation would make pill-like have three consonants together, which would be awkward.]

counterpart vs. **counter-revolutionary** [lack of hyphenation would make counter-revolutionary have two consonants together, which would be awkward.]

3. Use a hyphen when combining compound words when the second word begins with a capital letter.

Examples:

anti-American

non-Catholic

pre-Civil War

9-B   Compound Adjectives

1. When a compound adjective precedes the noun it modifies, use a hyphen to connect it (except if the first word ends in -ly).

Examples:

She was a **well-developed, well-nourished, under-educated** girl of 18.

She had a right **high-frequency** nerve loss.

It was a **normal-appearing** suture.

He was thought to be a **soft-spoken** man.

They were **fast-healing** wounds.

But: It was a slowly draining abscess. [the first word of the compound adjective ends in -ly.]

2. When a compound adjective follows the noun it modifies, do not use a hyphen.

Examples:

The baby was **well developed**.

Her fever was **low grade**.

The cocci was **gram negative**.

9-C   A Rule for Compound Prepositions

Usually separate clauses including compound prepositions from the rest of a sentence with a comma.

Examples:

In addition to medications, the patient was given diet modifications.

Over the course of a day, all the symptoms were gone.

9-D   Additional Rules for Compound Words

1. Compound words using the prefixes of **self-** and **all-**, or the suffixes **-elect** and -**free** should always be hyphenated.

    Examples:

self-control	**all**-encompassing
self-image	**all**-inclusive
self-controlled	**all**-Pro
president-**elect**	sympton-**free**

2. Use hyphenation to clarify meaning, to make pronunciation easier and with compound words including abbreviations.

    Examples:

    a **small bowel loop** [a bowel loop that is little in size] vs.

    a **small-bowel loop** [a loop of the small bowel of the intestine]

    post-traumatic [instead of posttraumatic]

    post-CABG

9-E   Special Rules for the Compound Words *Follow-up, Work-up* and *Check-up*

1. When the word is a verb, do not hyphenate.

    Examples:

    He is to **follow up** next week.

    She will **check up** the infant in a month.

    All his symptoms were **worked up**.

2. When the word is an adjective or noun, hyphenate.

Examples:

The patient is to be seen in **follow-up** next week.

The child was in for her **check-up**.

The doctor gave the girl a thorough **work-up**.

Note: **Workup**, without hyphenation, is acceptable when the compound is an adjective or noun.

9-F   General Rules for Hyphenation

1.   Use hyphens for written fractions or compound numbers.

Examples:

She drank **one-fifth** of a bottle of liquor.

There was a **two-thirds** majority vote.

She is to reduce the dosage by **one-half**. [or, She is to reduce the dosage by a half.]

2.   Use hyphens when spelling out the numbers twenty-one to ninety-nine.

Examples:

Twenty-one sagittal slices of the skull were made on CT scan.

Seventy-nine percent of patients with this condition improve in a year or less.

3.   Use hyphens when forming coined compound words.

Examples:

The patient is to stop taking **over-the-counter** nasal sprays.

He had a **ready-to-go** demeanor.

The physician developed a **watch-and-wait** attitude.

4.   Use hyphens when attaching some prefixes and suffixes (also, see compound words above).

Examples:

The patient's speech was very **un-American**.

He was wearing a **V-neck** sweater.

5.   Use hyphens with suture sizes including 0's.

Examples:

The wound was closed with **3-0** Prolene.

She used running **2-0** absorbable sutures for the subcutaneous tissue.

6. Use hyphens when expressing ranges in numbers that are in numeral form (when the numbers in the ranges are spelled out, however, use the word "to" instead of a hyphen).

Examples:

The patient was to have the wound rechecked every **7-10** days.

The WBCs were between **24,000-48,000**.

The operation's cost was in the ballpark of **$1,500-$2,500**.

But: She has had the symptoms for **two to three** days.

Unit 10

Contractions and Shortened Word Forms

Overview: Contractions are condensed forms of expressions. An apostrophe usually replaces the missing letters. Although in medical transcription contractions should generally not be used, it is helpful to know the correct forms of contractions. Shortened word forms are used commonly in medical records dictation, although some dictated brief forms are not acceptable in transcription. Use the following as a guide for contractions and shortened word forms:

10-A   General Rules for Contractions in Medical Transcription

1. Try to avoid contractions in medical transcription. If the client you are transcribing for permits, contractions may be used in informal records transcription such as office chart notes. However, when a physician dictates a contraction in formal correspondence, such as letters, use the words that form the contraction instead of the contraction.

2. Be careful not to confuse contractions with plurals and possessives. In a contraction, there are missing letters when two or more words are combined. In a plural case, no letters are missing, but an "s" or an " 's" is added to make a single word or group of words plural. In a possessive case, no letters are missing, but an " 's" or simply an apostrophe is added to make a single word or group of words express ownership or possession. Also, do not confuse the personal pronouns "its", "their", "your" and "whose" with the contractions "it's", "they're", "you're" and "who's".

3. Contractions of verb phrases (don't, weren't, isn't, aren't, etc.) are common in informal writing, but try not to use them in medical transcription; write out do not, were not, is not, are not, etc., whenever possible.

10-B   Examples of Contractions that Take an Apostrophe

it is → it's	were not → weren't
they are → they're	cannot → can't

you are → you're	1988 → '88
who is → who's	of the clock → o'clock
does not → doesn't	madam → ma'am

10-C   Examples of Contractions that Do Not Take an Apostrophe

all + together → altogether	through → thru
all + ready → already	until → till
all + though → although	

10-D   Special Rules for Some Contractions that Do Not Take an Apostrophe

1. Sometimes there is confusion whether or not to use a contraction when combining "all +" word combinations. If the word "all" means "each and every one," it should not become part of a contraction and should remain a single word.

   Examples:

   We were **all together**. *vs*. We were not **altogether** sure of our reasoning. [In the first sentence "all together" means all of us were gathered in one place; in the second sentence "altogether" means entirely or totally]

   We are **all ready** for the photo. *vs*. We had **already** discussed the matter. [In the first sentence "all ready" means all prepared or thoroughly prepared; in the second sentence "already" means prior to the current time or before now]

2. There is no contraction for the words "all right" and "a lot". These word groups should always be written as two words.

10-E   Shortened Word (Brief) Forms

1. Acceptable brief forms — The following shortened or brief word forms are usually acceptable, except if dictated in full form or if the physician's or hospital's style necessitates it to be written out in full form.

exam → examination	Pap smear → Papanicolaou's test
lab → laboratory	postop → postoperative
prepped → prepared	sed rate → sedimentation rate
prep → prepare	flu → Hemophilus influenzae

preop → preoperative   pro time → prothrombin time

Strep → Streptococcus   Staph → Staphylococcus

2.   Unacceptable brief forms — Do not use brief forms for the following words; always spell out the complete word.

subcutaneous/subcuticular (subcu)	palpable or palpation (palp)
laparotomy/laparoscopy (lap)	capsules/capital letters (caps)
temperature (temp)	tablets (tabs)
electrolytes (lytes)	prescription (script)
calculated (calc)	vital signs (vitals)
differential (diff)	chemical (chem)
appendectomy (appy)	medications/medicines (meds)
dexamethasone (dex)	saturation (sat)
bilirubin (bili)	audiogram/audiology (audio)

Unit 11

Abbreviations

Overview: Abbreviations are shortened forms of words. Some use periods, some use capital letters standing alone, and some use both periods and small letters. Abbreviations are commonly used in medical transcription, and you should thoroughly familiarize yourself with the proper forms of abbreviations and some common forms they can take.

11-A   General Rules

1. **Do** use abbreviations:

    - with most quantity measurements (e.g., 24 cm, 1 g, 10 lb., etc.)

    - with most laboratory data (e.g., BUN, CBC, SMAC, ESR, etc.) [see Appendix D]

    - with Latin abbreviations (such as e.g., etc., i.e., et al.) (also, always use commas before and after these abbreviations)

    - when the numeral directly precedes the unit of measure (e.g., 15%, but 15 mg percent)

    - when expressing units measurements including "per" with a slash (e.g., 15 mm/dl, or 15 mm per day)

2.

    - in diagnoses, impressions, assessments or in the names of operative procedures

    - at the beginning of a sentence

    - in measurements, when the quantity is unknown (e.g., abbreviate milligrams in 1 mg or 3 cm, do not abbreviate "several milligrams," "a few centimeters," etc.)

    - if the abbreviation is not dictated (e.g., if "total abdominal hysterectomy/bilateral salpingo-oophorectomy" is dictated, do not abbreviate it TAH-BSO)

- with days of the week or names of months

- on the first reference of most companies' names, organizations, and on the first reference to genus name (e.g., the first reference to "TENS unit" you should type "transcutaneous electrical nerve stimulation unit," or with "H. influenza" on first reference you should type "Hemophilus influenzae")

- with certain laboratory data (e.g., eosinophils, reticulocytes, differential, hemoglobin and hematocrit, etc.) [see Appendix D]

- with most chemical symbols, such as K for potassium, Pb for lead, C for carbon, etc., when they are not part of laboratory data (however, O_2 and all forms and combinations including oxygen are acceptable to abbreviate everywhere but in a diagnosis)

11-B   Specific Abbreviation Usage — Uppercase Abbreviations

1. Usually capitalized abbreviations do not take periods in their forms. When they are made plural, a simple lowercase "s" should be added, not apostrophe + "s" ('s). Capitalize the following when they are abbreviated (* preceding an abbreviation denotes it should be spelled out, when possible):

   AB — abortio (# of aborted pregnancies); abortion

   * A/B — acid/base (ratio)

   * ACL — anterior cruciate ligament

   * ABG — arterial blood gas

   ADA — American Diabetic Association

   * AKA — above the knee amputation; also known as; alcoholic ketoacidosis

   * AMA — American Medical Association; Against Medical Advice

   ANA — antinuclear antibody

   * A&P — anterior and posterior; auscultation and percussion; assessment and plan

   * ASA — aspirin

   ASAP — as soon as possible

   ASCVD — arteriosclerotic cardiovascular disease

   * BBB — bundle branch block

   * BCP — birth control pills

BE — barium enema

* BKA — below the knee amputation

* BP — blood pressure

* BPD — biparietal diameter; bronchopulmonary dysplasia

BPH — benign prostatic hypertrophy

BSER — brainstem evoked response

BUN — blood urea nitrogen

* BUS — Bartholin, urethral and Skene's glands

* CA — carcinoma

CABG — coronary artery bypass graft

CAT — computerized axial tomography

CBC — complete blood count

CEA — carcinoembryonic antigen

CHD — congenital heart disease

CHF — congestive heart failure

CNS — central nervous system

COPD — chronic obstructive pulmonary disease

CPAP — continuous positive airway pressure

* CPD — cephalopelvic disproportion

CPR — cardiopulmonary resuscitation

* C&S — culture and sensitivity

* CSF — cerebrospinal fluid

CT — computerized tomography

* CVA — cerebrovascular accident; costovertebral angle

D&C — dilatation and curettage

DDD — degenerative disc disease

DES — diethylstilbestrol

DJD — degenerative joint disease

DO — doctor of osteopathy

* DOE — dyspnea on exertion

DPT — diphtheria, pertussis and tetanus immunization

DT — diphtheria/tetanus; delirium tremens

DTR — deep tendon reflex

ECG — electrocardiogram; echocardiogram

* ECT — electroconvulsive therapy

* ED — emergency department

EDC — estimated date of confinement

EEG — electroencephalogram

EG — esophagogastric

EGD — esophagogastroduodenoscopy

EKG — electrocardiogram (also ECG)

EMG — electromyography

ENG — electronystagmography

* ENT — ears, nose and throat (otorhinolaryngo-)

* EOM(I) — extraocular movements (intact)

ER — emergency room

ESP — extrasensory perception

* ESR — erythrocyte sedimentation rate

ET — endotracheal

* ETOH — ethanol; alcohol

* FB — foreign body

FBS — fasting blood sugar

FSH — follicle stimulating hormone; facioscapulohumeral

* G — gravida (# of pregnancies)

* GC — gonococcus

GI — gastrointestinal

* GP — general practitioner

GU — genitourinary

GYN — gynecology

HCG — human chorionic gonadotropin

HCT — hematocrit

* HCTZ — hydrochlorothiazide

HEENT — head, ears, eyes, nose and throat

HGB — hemoglobin

* H&H — hemoglobin and hematocrit

HIV — human immunodeficiency virus

HMO — health maintenance organization

* H&P — History and Physical (Examination)

* HPI — history of the present illness

IAC — internal auditory canal

ICU — intensive care unit

* I&D — incision and drainage

IM — intramuscular

* I&O — intake(s) and output(s)

IPPB — intermittent positive pressure breathing

IQ — intelligence quotient

IU — international units

IUD — intrauterine contraceptive device

IV — intravenous

IVP — intravenous pyelogram

JVD — jugular venous distention

KOH — potassium hydroxide

KUB — kidney, ureter and bladder (x-ray)

LLL — left lower lobe (lung)

LLQ — left lower quadrant (abdomen)

* LMP — last menstrual period

LS — lumbosacral

L/S — lecithin/sphingomyelin ratio

LUL — left upper lobe

LUQ — left upper quadrant

MCP — metacarpophalangeal (joint)

MI — myocardial infarction; mitral insufficiency

* MMK — Marshall-Marchetti-Krantz (procedure)

MRI — magnetic resonance imaging

MS — multiple sclerosis

NG — nasogastric

* NKA — no known allergies

NPH — Isophane insulin

NSAID — nonsteroidal anti-inflammatory drug

NST — nonstress test

OB — obstetrics

* OBS — organic brain syndrome

OCD — obsessive-compulsive disorder

* O&P — ova and parasites

OR — operating room

* ORIF — open reduction and internal fixation

OTC — over-the-counter (medication)

* P — para (# of live births)

PA — posterior-anterior

PAC — premature atrial contraction

PAT — paroxysmal atrial tachycardia

* PCN — penicillin

* PE — pulmonary embolus; peripheral edema; pleural effusion;
pharyngoesophageal; physical examination

PEEP — positive end-expiratory pressure

* PERRLA — pupils equal, round and reactive to light and
accommodation

PID — pelvic inflammatory disease

* PMI — point of maximum impulse

* PND — paroxysmal nocturnal dyspnea

* PROM — premature rupture of membranes; passive range of motion

* PTA — prior to admission

PVC — premature ventricular contraction

QA — quality assurance

RBC — red blood count; red blood cell

REM — rapid eye movement

RLL — right lower lobe

RLQ — right lower quadrant

R/O — rule out

ROS — Review of Systems (part of H&P report)

RUL — right upper lobe

RUQ — right upper quadrant

SAB — spontaneous abortion

SCM — sternoclcidomastoid

SI — international system (units); sacroiliac

SIDS — sudden infant death syndrome

SMAC — superior mesenteric artery count

* SR — sedimentation rate; sinus rhythm

SSS — sick sinus syndrome

STD — sexually transmitted disease

* T&A — tonsillectomy and adenoidectomy

TAB — therapeutic abortion

TAH-BSO — total abdominal hysterectomy/bilateral salpingo-oophorectomy

* TB — tuberculosis

TIA — transient ischemic attack

TM — tympanic membrane

TMJ — temporomandibular joint

TSH — thyroid stimulating hormone

TURP — transurethral resection of the prostate

* UA — urinalysis

UGI — upper gastrointestinal tract series

UPPP — uvulopalatopharyngoplasty

URI — upper respiratory infection

UTI — urinary tract infection

UV — ureterovesical; ultraviolet

VBAC — vaginal birth after cesarean

VD — venereal disease

VDRL — Venereal Disease Research Laboratories test

VQ — ventilation/perfusion lung scan

WBC — white blood count; white blood cell

* WNL — within normal limits

* XRT — x-ray therapy (radiotherapy)

* YO — year-old

2.   Also, usually use capitalized abbreviations when used with numbers:

2PD — two point discrimination

5FU — 5-fluorouracil

3D — three dimensional

11-C   Specific Abbreviation Usage — Lowercase Abbreviations

1.   Usually lowercase abbreviations take periods in their forms, except in the case of units of measurement. When they are made plural, the periods should be deleted and an apostrophe + "s" should be added ('s). You should use lowercase with the following when they are abbreviated (abbreviations with asterisks preceding them should be spelled out, when possible):

a.c. — before meals or food	h. — hour
* a.d. — right ear	h.s. — at the hour of sleep
a.m. — morning (ante meridiem)	n.p.o. — nothing by mouth
* a.s. — left ear (also a.l.)	* o.d. — right eye
* a.u. — both ears	o.s. — left eye (also o.l.)
b.i.d. — twice a day	p.c. — after meals
d. — day	* o.u. — both eyes

p.m. — afternoon (post meridiem)	q.h. — every hour
p.o. — by mouth (orally)	q.i.d. — four times daily
p.r.n. — as needed	q.o.d. — every other day
q.d. — every day	t.i.d. — three times a day

2. Latin abbreviations are usually lowercase and take periods. These abbreviations should be preceded and followed by commas when used in writing. The following are some common Latin abbreviations:

cf. — compare

e.g. — for example

etc. — and so forth; and other things

et seq. — and the following

et al. — and others (often used in source citations)

i.e. — that is; in other words

ibid. — in the same place (often used to indicate the same book or page in source citations)

id. — the same (often used to indicate repetition of an author's name or title in source citations)

11-D   Specific Abbreviation Usage — Mixed Case Abbreviations

Usually mixed case abbreviations do not take periods in their forms. Many chemical symbols also use mixed case (see Figure 21). When mixed case abbreviations are made plural, add a simple lowercase "s" if the abbreviation ends in an upper case letter, or add an apostrophe + "s" ('s) if the abbreviation ends in a lower case letter. Use a combination of upper and lower case with the following abbreviations, as demonstrated (abbreviations with asterisks preceding them should be spelled out, when possible):

* Bx — biopsy

* Cx — cervix; cancel

  dB — decibel

* Dx — diagnosis

  ECoG — electrocochleogram

* Fx — fracture

* Hx — history

  Hz — hertz

FIGURE 21   Common Chemical Symbols (Atomic Elements)

Symbol	Chemical Name	Symbol	Chemical Name
Ag	silver	K	potassium
Al	aluminum	Kr	krypton
Am	americium	Li	lithium
Ar	argon	Mo	molybdenum
As	arsenic	N	nitrogen
Au	gold	Na	sodium
Ba	barium	Ne	neon
Be	beryllium	Ni	nickel
Bi	bismuth	O	oxygen
B	boron	P	phosphorus
Br	bromine	Pb	lead
C	carbon	Pt	platinum
Ca	calcium	Pu	plutonium
Cd	cadmium	Ra	radium
Ce	cerium	Rh	rhodium
Cl	chlorine	Rn	radon
Co	cobalt	S	sulfur
Cr	chromium	Sb	antimony
Cs	cesium	Se	selenium
Cu	coppper	Si	silicon
Er	erbium	Sn	tin
F	fluorine	Tc	technetium
Fe	iron	Te	tellurium
Fr	francium	Ti	titanium
Ga	gallium	Tl	thallium
Gd	gadolinium	U	uranium
H	hydrogen	W	tungsten
He	helium	Xe	xenon
Hg	mercury	Y	yttrium
I	iodine	Yb	ytterbium
Ir	iridium	Zn	zinc
Mg	magnesium	Zr	zirconium
Mn	manganese		

IgA — immunoglobulin A

IgD — immunoglobulin D

IgE — immunoglobulin E

IgG — immunoglobulin G

IgM — immunoglobulin M

Kcal — kilocalorie

mEq — milliequivalent

mHz — megahertz

mmHg — millimeters of mercury

mRNA — messenger ribonucleic acid

MyG — myasthenia gravis

pH — hydrogen ion concentration

* Px — prognosis

Rh factor — Rhesus factor in blood sampling

* Rx — prescription; pharmacy

tRNA — transfer ribonucleic acid

* Tx — treatment; therapy; transfusion

11-E   Units of Measure

Usually metric unit abbreviations use lowercase or capital and lower case without periods. Usually English (avoirdupois) measurement units use lower-case abbreviations with periods.

Metric

ng, nl, nm — nanogram, nanoliter, nanometer

mcg, mcl, mcm — microgram, microliter, micrometer

mg, ml, mm — milligram, milliliter, millimeter

cg, cl, cm — centigram, centiliter, centimeter

dg, dl, dm — decigram, deciliter, decimeter

g, l, m — gram, liter, meter

Dg, Dl, Dm — dekagram, dekaliter, dekameter

hg, hl, hm — hectogram, hectoliter, hectometer

kg, kl, km — kilogram, kiloliter, kilometer

English

gr. — grain	hr. — hour
oz. — ounce	min. — minute
lb. — pound	sec. — second
pt. — pint	ft. — foot
qt. — quart	in. — inch
gal. — gallon	yd. — yard
tsp. — teaspoon	mi. — mile
tbsp. — tablespoon	

11-F   Abbreviations with Temperatures

It is appropriate to use only the numeral to indicate degrees, if dictated. However, if either the word "degrees" or the words "Fahrenheit" or "Celsius" are used, both the word "degrees" and the type, either Fahrenheit or Celsius, must be written. So, a temperature of 100 in a febrile patient would be written either "temperature was 100" or "temperature was 100 degrees Fahrenheit," but not "temperature was 100 degrees" or "temperature was 100 Fahrenheit."

11-G   Abbreviations with Geographic Names

In correspondence (letters), use abbreviations for direction (S., N., E., W.), street (Ave., Dr., St., Cir., Blvd.), state (use the postal abbreviations, such as CA [not Calif.], CO, TX, IA, ME, etc.), and country (U.S.A., USSR, R.O.C.) if there is an acceptable abbreviation for the country. Commas precede and follow all cities with states (e.g., She has lived in Denver, Colorado, for three years). In formal reports, do not use geographic abbreviations.

11-H   Abbreviations with Dates

Write out days of the week and dates (Monday, January 19, 1989, instead of Mon., Jan. 19, '89 or Mon., 1/19/89). Commas precede and follow all dates. Use dashes instead of slashes with dates (1-19-89), unless it is the preferred style of the physician or hospital to do otherwise. Do not use ordinals (numbers used to show sequence in a series, such as 12th), except when they precede the month or stand alone (e.g., the 12th of March, or the 12th, but not March 12th).

11-I   Abbreviations with Titles and Degrees

1. Always abbreviate social (courtesy) titles when they are used with names. Drop the courtesy title if a professional title is used.

    Examples:

    Mrs. Indira Khan, or Indira Khan, R.N.

    Ms. Linda Jones or **Dr. Linda Jones,** or Linda Jones, Ph.D.

    Mr. Lin Chang, or Lin Chang, M.A.

    Dr. Felix Delgado, or Felix Delgado, Ph.D

2. Never use both a social title before a name and a professional title afterwards concurrently.

    Examples:

    Joe Littlebear, M.D. or Dr. Joe Littlebear, not **Dr. Joe Littlebear, M.D.**

    Luci Kamchatka, P.A.-C. or Ms. Luci Kamchatka, not Ms. Luci Kamchatka, P.A.-C.

3. Use periods and no space when using a professional title.

    Examples:

    Kim Miyaki, M.D.

    Sue Smith, R.N.

    Hanna Johansen, R.M.T.

    Tasha Mutombe, B.A., M.A., Ph.D., M.D. (always use the degree with the least educational requirements first)

4. Abbreviate these social titles when used before a name: **Dr. (doctor), Gov. (governor), Lt. Gov. (lieutenant governor), Mr. (mister), Mrs. (mistress), Rep. (representative), Sen. (senator), Lt. (lieutenant), Col. (colonel), the Rev. (the Reverend),** etc.

11-J   Abbreviations with Names, Sign-off Initials and Letter Notations

Use the following as a guide:

J. P. Getty, not J.P. Getty or JP Getty

RH/jmts1, RH:jmts1 or jmts1, not rh:JMTS1 or rh:jmts1

pc: (photocopy to) or cc: (carbon copy to), not PC or CC

Encl. or Enclosures, not Enc.

Unit 12

Capitalization

Overview: Should most abbreviations be capitalized? When do you capitalize words following a colon? A skilled transcriptionist must need to know the answers to these and other questions about capitalization. The following is a guide to when to, and when not to, use capitalization.

12-A *Capitalize the first letter of the first word of every complete sentence.*

> *Examples*:
>
> Two percent Xylocaine with epinephrine was used in the appendectomy.
>
> Examination of cranial nerves II through XII is not remarkable.
>
> Fifty-five out of one-hundred patients do not develop the symptoms.

12-B *Capitalize proper nouns, proper adjectives and other proper words.*

> *Examples*:
>
> The patient, John Smith, lived in Los Angeles, California.
>
> Madame Curie was a French scientist.
>
> Her Babinski's reflexes were normal.

12-C *Capitalize the entire heading for a formal subject heading, and capitalize only the first letters of all words in a subheading. Capitalize only the first letter of the first word of subheadings following a formal heading.*

> *Examples*:
>
> HISTORY OF PRESENT ILLNESS: The patient is a 32-year-old. . .
>
> Family History: The patient's mother died at age 59 of a. . .
>
> PHYSICAL EXAMINATION: Vital signs: Temperature 100, pulse 80, respirations 24 and blood pressure 140/90.

12-D   Guidelines for Heading Capitalization

Use the following as a guide for how to capitalize section headings for the six major reports:

<u>HISTORY AND PHYSICAL</u>

    CHIEF COMPLAINT:

    HISTORY OF PRESENT ILLNESS: (or, SUBJECTIVE:)

    PAST HISTORY:

        Past Medical History:

        Family History:

        Social History/Habits:

    REVIEW OF SYSTEMS:

        Skin:

        Head, Eyes, Ears, Nose and Throat:

        Mouth:

        Neck:

        Chest:

        Lungs:

        Heart:

        Abdomen:

        Extremities: (or, Musculoskeletal:)

        Neurologic:

    PHYSICAL EXAMINATION: (or, OBJECTIVE:)

        (same subheadings as in Review of Systems)

    LABORATORY DATA:

    IMPRESSION: (or, DIAGNOSIS: or, ASSESSMENT:)

    PLAN:

<u>CONSULTATION</u>

    DATE OF CONSULTATION:

    REASON FOR CONSULTATION:

    (the primary data for the consultation needs no heading)

ASSESSMENT:

RECOMMENDATIONS:

PATHOLOGY REPORT

TISSUE SUBMITTED:

GROSS:

MICROSCOPIC:

IMPRESSION:

OPERATIVE REPORT

PREOPERATIVE DIAGNOSIS:

POSTOPERATIVE DIAGNOSIS:

OPERATION(S) PERFORMED:

FINDINGS AND PROCEDURE:

Sponge count:

Estimated blood loss:

RADIOLOGY REPORT

(PROCEDURE NAME)   DATE:

IMPRESSION:

DISCHARGE SUMMARY

DATE OF ADMISSION:

DATE OF DISCHARGE:

ADMITTING DIAGNOSIS:

CONSULTATIONS:

PROCEDURES:

HISTORY:

Past History:

PHYSICAL EXAMINATION:

LABORATORY DATA:

HOSPITAL COURSE:

DISCHARGE DIAGNOSIS(ES):

12-E   *When listing components of systems in the review of systems or physical examination, capitalize only the first letters of words following periods. (It is not necessary to use complete sentences in the review of systems and the physical examination.)*

Examples:

Eyes: Clear. Pupils equal, round and reactive to light and accommodation; fundi normal; conjunctivae normal.

Chest: Clear. No rhonchi, rales or rubs. There are no abnormal lung sounds.

Heart: Normal sinus rhythm.

12-F   *Place a capitalized article, pronoun or title before words that are usually not capitalized. (Also, always insert an article before the word "patient" whenever it is dictated alone in a sentence.)*

Examples:

Mr. vanHuesen arrived well before his appointment time.

The pH was 7.6; however, the specific gravity was 1.001.

The patient was seen in his office.

12-G   *Capitalize "I" when used as a pronoun and "O" when used as an interjection.*

Examples:

The patient stated he was sick; however, **I** had my doubts.

The song, "**O** Holy Night," rekindled old memories for the patient.

12-H   *Capitalize the first letter of formal names of races, nationalities and languages, but do not capitalize informal descriptions of race by color.*

Examples:

The patient was a Caucasian female who spoke German fluently.

He was a soft-spoken, black male, who was in no acute distress.

She was a well-developed, well-nourished, Oriental woman.

12-I   *Capitalize the first letter of a word following a colon only when the word stands alone or when the word begins a complete sentence. When there is a clause or phrase following a colon that further explains text before the colon, it is not necessary to capitalize the first word of the clause or phrase.*

> *Examples*:
>
> Genitourinary examination: Normal.
>
> Family History: Noncontributory.
>
> Past History: The patient had the usual childhood illnesses. He had a tonsillectomy at age 8 and an adenoidectomy at age 9.
>
> The patient had the following complaints: nausea, diaphoresis, and two-pillow orthopnea.

12-J   *Capitalize the first letter of formal names of diseases, eponyms (diseases named after a person) and the genus, group or family name of disease processes, but do not capitalize informal disease processes.*

> *Examples*:
>
> DISCHARGE DIAGNOSES:
>
> 1.   Chronic Hemophilus influenzae.
>
> 2.   Past history of Crohn's disease.
>
> 3.   Status post myocardial infarction.
>
> 4.   Chronic diabetes mellitus.
>
> 5.   End-stage leukemia.

12-K   *Capitalize the first letter of the first word of these common genus and species names:*

> Actinomyces   Ex.:   Actinomyces muris
>
> Amoeba   Ex.:   Amoeba urinae granulata
>
> Aspergillus   Ex.:   Aspergillus auricularis
>
> Bacillus   Ex.:   Bacillus proteus
>
> Bacteroides   Ex.:   Bacteroides fragilis
>
> Borrelia   Ex.:   Borrelia hispanica

Campylobacter	Ex.: Campylobacter fetus
Candida	Ex.: Candida albicans
Cellvibrio	Ex.: Cellvibrio fulvus
Chromobacterium	Ex.: Chromobacterium amythistinum
Clostridium	Ex.: Clostridium difficile
Corynebacterium	Ex.: Corynebacterium hoagii
Cysticercus	Ex.: Cysticercus ovis
Diplococcus	Ex.: Diplococcus pneumoniae
Echinostoma	Ex.: Echinostoma melis
Endomyces	Ex.: Endomyces capsulatus
Entamoeba	Ex.: Entamoeba tropicalis
Enterobacter	Ex.: Enterobacter cloacae
Escherichia	Ex.: Escherichia coli
Filaria	Ex.: Filaria labialis
Hemophilus	Ex.: Hemophilus influenzae
Hermodendrum	Ex.: Hermodendrum rossicum
Herpes (virus)	Ex.: Herpes zoster
Klebsiella	Ex.: Klebsiella oxytoca
Lactobacillus	Ex.: Lactobacillus fermenti
Microsporum	Ex.: Microsporum fulvum
Monilia	Ex.: Monilia sitophila
Mycobacterium	Ex.: Mycobacterium microti
Mycoplasma	Ex.: Mycoplasma buccale
Neisseria	Ex.: Neisseria mucosa
Peptococcus	Ex.: Peptococcus magnus
Proteus	Ex.: Proteus filamenta
Pseudomonas	Ex.: Pseudomonas aeruginosa
Saccharomyces	Ex.: Saccharomyces capillitii
Salmonella	Ex.: Salmonella typhosa
Serratia	Ex.: Serratia indica

Shigella	Ex.: Shigella dysenteriae
Staphylococcus	Ex.: Staph aureus
Streptococcus	Ex.: Strep faecalis
Taenia	Ex.: Taenia lata
Treponema	Ex.: Treponema orale
Trichomonas	Ex.: Trichomonas vaginalis

12-L *Key sentences describing patient allergies either in bold print or in all capitals when the allergies are noted in the history.*

Examples:

She is allergic to penicillin and codeine. She has no other complaints.

The patient is up to date on his immunizations. HE IS ALLERGIC TO ASPIRIN.

12-M *Usually capitalize Roman numerals. Use lowercase Roman numerals only as subnumerals when outlining a report, research paper, etc.*

Examples:

a.   Cranial nerves **II** through **XII** were intact. She was gravida I para I AB 0.

b.   I.   Common symptoms

   A.   Subjective

      1.   Headache

      2.   Stomach ache

      3.   Nausea

      4.   Painful musculoskeletal area

         a.   limb

            i.   arm

            ii.   leg

            iii.   hand

            iv.   foot

         b.   spine

                              B.   Objective

                                    1.   Vomiting

                                    2.   Diarrhea

                        II.   Not so common symptoms

                              A.   Thrombosis

                              B.   Hemorrhage

                              C.   Cyanosis

12-N   *Capitalize trade or brand names, especially of drugs. (Consult the PDR or a drug index for further information on which drugs to capitalize.)*

   Examples:

   The discharge medications were: Dyazide, hydrochlorothiazide, aspirin, Tylenol, erythromycin and Maalox.

   Motrin is a brand name for ibuprofen.

   She is to take Pen-Vee K twice a day for two weeks.

12-O   *Capitalize most abbreviations. WIth lowercase abbreviations, use periods between the letters. Capitalize abbreviations used in geographical directions.*

   Examples:

   The CBC showed 7,900 WBCs and 300 RBCs.

   Her rhinitis medicamentosa was treated with steroids p.r.n.

   The patient's address was 15 S. Main Street.

12-P   *Do not capitalize the following:*

   a.   names of relationships, unless they substitute for proper names

   Examples:

   The patient's aunt was present.

   His mom was also quite helpful.

   He remembered Father.

   b.   names of hospital or medical departments, specialties, or hospital rooms, unless they include the entire hospital name

Examples:

The patient arrived via ambulance at the **Mercy Hospital Emergency Room**, and she was taken to the intensive **care unit** at that time.

Dr. Yoko Nitobe, orthopedist, performed a consultation.

The patient was sent for an **ophthalmology** evaluation.

c.   Greek letters

Examples:

alpha

beta-lactamase

gamma rays

d.   units of measure

Examples:

There were 3 **mg** of fluid.

The infant weighed 7 **lb.**, 6 **oz.**

The Discharge Summary took 250 **Kb** of space.

e.   a.m. or p.m.

Examples:

The patient arrived to the ER at 12:00 **p.m.**

She was placed on a regimen of **a.m.** diuretics.

f.   most abbreviations relating to medications

Examples:

take two tablets **q.i.d.** x 3 days

take 10 tsp. at **h.s. p.r.n.**

Unit 13

Plural and Possessive Forms

Overview: Plural and possessive forms are often confused. Knowing how to make English words plural is difficult, and knowing how to make medical words plural is even harder. Many times a physician dictates the singular form of a word that should be plural, incorrectly pronounces the plural word, or gives punctuation instructions that would make the word possessive. The possessive case shows possession or ownership of someone or something by someone or something else. Possession can be expressed either with a clause containing "of", or with an apostrophe or an apostrophe + "s". Following are some rules and aids for making words plural and possessive.

13-A   Rules for American (non Latin or Greek) Words

1. For most words, simply add "s".

    Examples:

    pill → pills

    symptom → symptoms

    ear → ears

2. For most words ending in "z", "s", "x", "ch" or "sh", add "es".

    Examples:

    tax → taxes

    search → searches

    brush → brushes

    buzz → buzzes

    gas → gases

3. For words ending in "y", if the "y" is preceded by a consonant change the "y" to "i" and add "es".

Examples:

extremity → extremities

study → studies

disparity → disparities

dichotomy → dichotomies

4. For words ending in "y", if the "y" is preceded by a vowel add "s".

    Examples:

    key → keys

    delay → delays

    journey → journeys

    attorney → attorneys

13-B   Rules for Latin or Greek or Latin- or Greek-based Words

1. For words ending in "x", change the "x" to "c" or "g" and add "es".

    Examples:

    calyx → calyces or calices

    hallux → halluces

    apex → apices

    meninx → meninges

2. For words ending in "a", keep the "a" and add "e".

    Examples:

    antenna → antennae

    larva → larvae

    petechia → petechiae

    stria → striae

3. For words ending in "is" drop the "is" and add "es" or "ides".

    Examples:

    diagnosis → diagnoses

    metamorphosis → metamorphoses

prosthesis → prosthe**ses**

testis → test**es**

epididymis → epididym**ides**

4. For words ending in "um", drop the "um" and add "a".

   Examples:

   diverticulum → diverticul**a**

   datum → dat**a**

   agendum → agend**a**

   bacterium → bacteri**a**

5. For words ending in "us", drop the "us" and add "i" (notable exceptions are "virus" and "sinus", where you add "es").

   Examples:

   anulus → anul**i**

   alumnus → alumn**i**

   calculus → calcul**i**

   fundus → fund**i**

6. For words ending in "en", drop the "en" and add "ina".

   Examples:

   lumen → lum**ina**

   semen → sem**ina**

   velamen → velam**ina**

   foramen → foram**ina**

7. For words ending in "on", drop the "on" and add "a".

   Examples:

   phenomenon → phenomen**a**

   ganglion → gangli**a**

   criterion → criteri**a**

8. For words ending in "oma", change the "oma" to "omata".

   Examples:

adenoma → aden**omata**

condyloma → condy**lomata**

fibroma → fibr**omata**

9. For words ending in "u", change the "u" to "ua".

Examples:

cornu → corn**ua**

genu → gen**ua**

13-C   Special Plural Cases

1. For plurals of single letters, numbers, words named as words, or lower case abbreviations, add an apostrophe + "s" (also, drop the periods when making lower case abbreviations plural).

Examples:

The surgery would be performed; there would be no **if's, and's** or **but's.**

On speech evaluation, the patient had difficulty pronouncing his **L's, R's** and **Th's.**

There are two **6's** in 1966. Everyone knows the **1960's** were wild.

The patient could tolerate the n.p.o. diets, but he had trouble tolerating the **po's.**

2. For plurals of compound words that contain only equal nouns or nouns and verbs, make only the last word of the compound plural.

Examples:

There was one nurse practitioner present. → There were many nurse practitioner**s present.**

The patient had a breakthrough in his prophylaxis. → The patient had several breakthrough**s** in his prophylaxis.

A cross-match was done of the child's blood. → Two cross-match**es** were done of the child's blood.

3. For plurals of compound words that contain unequal nouns or nouns along with other parts of speech such as prepositions, make only the main noun of the compound plural.

Examples:

His mother-in-law was in group therapy. → The mothers-in-law were in group therapy.

The chairman of the board held a meeting last night. → The co-chairmen of the board held a meeting last night.

There was a teaspoonful of medicine in the dropper. → There were three teaspoonsful of medicine in the dropper.

The accident would not have occurred at a speed of one mile-per-hour. → The accident occurred at a speed of 50 miles-per-hour.

4.   Do not change abbreviated units of measure when making them plural.

Examples:

191 **mg** of fluid

3 **lb.** of adipose

16 **oz.** of plasma

5.   When it is necessary to write out units of measure, add an "s" to make the word plural.

Examples:

There were many millimeters of fluid withdrawn.

The patient weighed several kilograms.

13-D   ***To form the possessive of singular or plural nouns that do not end in "s", add an apostrophe + "s".***

Examples:

The doctor's bill was extremely high.

The patient felt he was no one's relative.

The children's fevers were high.

The men's room is located at the end of the hall.

13-E   ***To form the possessive of singular nouns or names or that end in s, add an apostrophe + "s". (An exception to this rule is when a noun or name ends in an "s" or a "z" sound, or when a noun or name has more than one "s" sound, or when a noun or name sounds like it is already plural; in these cases, add only an apostrophe.)***

Examples:

Mr. Jones's physician lives in Vermont.

The gas's fumes were strong.

The calculus's edges were uneven.

Mr. Martinez' daughter signed the consent form. ["Martinez" ends in a "z" sound.]

The archaeologists thought they had found Ramses' tomb. ["Ramses" contains two "s" sounds.]

It was without question Mr. Bowles' handwriting. ["Bowles" sounds like it is already plural.]

13-F   **To form the possessive of plural nouns or names that end in "s", add only an apostrophe.**

Examples:

The otolaryngologists' symposium lasted one week.

The Joneses' daughter was out of town.

The pain was of three days' duration.

13-G   **To form the possessive of compound nouns or word groups, add an apostrophe + "s" to the last word.**

Examples:

The queen's lady-in-waiting's birthday was yesterday.

Accidentally the surgeon removed someone else's tonsils.

The president-elect's finance troubles were typical.

13-H   **If two or more words each individually show possession, add an apostrophe + "s" to each word.**

Examples:

Maria's, John's and Philip's diagnoses were similar.

The doctor's and nurse's courses were different but prepared each of them well.

13-1   *If two or more words each show joint possession, add an apostrophe + "s" to the last word only.*

     Examples:

     Invoices are the patient and the insurance company's responsibility.

     Jerry and Juan's task was to study for the American Red Cross exam.

Unit 14

Numbers and Number Combinations

Overview: Should you begin a sentence with a number? Do you use figures or written numbers when expressing a patient's age? These questions can be difficult to answer if you are not adept in how to use numbers and number combinations. Decisions as to whether to use Arabic numerals, Roman numerals or written numbers are constantly having to be made by medical transcriptionists. Use the following as a guide.

[All numerals are Arabic cardinal numbers, unless otherwise specified]

14-A *Use figures for numbers greater than nine, and spell out numbers one through nine (this rule is specific to transcribing medical records; the number "10" may be spelled out in other types of writing).*

Examples:

The patient was in the hospital for **five** days.

There were **100,000** platelets in the blood.

A deciliter consists of **10** liters.

14-B *Use a combination of figures and words to express numbers greater than 999,999.*

Examples:

The event included **10 million** people.

The **$5 billion** deficit would be hard to overcome.

Construction costs for the new wing of the hospital are around **$200 million**.

14-C *Use commas to separate thousands from hundreds.*

> *Examples:*
>
> There were **11,600** WBCs on the blood analysis.
>
> The pathologist found **210,000** platelets during the CBC.
>
> The white count was **8,900**.

14-D *Use words for numbers that begin sentences.*

> *Examples:*
>
> **Ten** percent Xylocaine was used for the operation.
>
> **One hundred and twenty-five** people were present at the symposium.
>
> **Fifteen thousand** colonies of bacteria were seen on culture.

14-E *When using several numbers together, either consistently spell them out or use figures.*

> *Examples:*
>
> The patient will be seen in follow-up in **7 to 10** days.
>
> **Seventy-five** people out of **one hundred** use this medication.
>
> Complications can occur between **three** and **seven** days.

14-F *Always use figures with ages (this rule is specific to transcribing medical records; ages may be spelled out in other types of writing).*

> *Examples:*
>
> The patient was **25** years old.
>
> She was a well-developed **9-year-old** child.
>
> The **1-month-old** baby had a sister **age 2**.

14-G *Use figures with most abbreviations, units of measure, laboratory data and symbols.*

> *Examples:*
>
> On CBC there were **5** bands, **35** lymphs and the pH was **6.5**.

An incision was made **5** cm superior to the peritoneum.

At **100** degrees Fahrenheit the reaction should be **50%** completed.

14-H   *Use zero in numerical figure form as a placeholder with decimals, and for consistency in an expression. Use a negative indefinite pronoun when possible to substitute for zero in an expression.*

Examples:

The patient was placed on Synthroid **0.25** mg.

The normal range for myeloblasts is **0.3-5.0%**.

There were **no** eosinophils present.

14-I   *Use fractions with quantities of age and english measure, and decimals with quantities of metric measure. Also, use figures with measurements including height, width and/or length, or in expressions using an "x" to represent "times" or "by".*

Examples:

She was a **9-6/12-year-old**, white female.

The jagged laceration was **2.5** cm in width x **3.5 cm** in length.

The patient's weight was **125-1/2 lb.**

Several **4 x 4's** were used in the building.

14-J   *Spell out fractions of less than one, but use figures with fractions greater than one.*

Examples:

The precipitate was decreased by **one-half** percent.

Of patients with this disease, **two-thirds** benefit from treatment.

His physician decreased the dosage by **one fourth**.

The condition lasted for **2-1/2** days.

14-K   *Spell out fractions when using the word "of" between the fraction and what it modifies; use figures for fractions when they are units of measure.*

>   *Examples:*
>
>   Less than **one-third** of all patients prefer this medication.
>
>   The syringe was filled with **1/2 cc** of Xylocaine.

14-L   *Use figures with + and - signs, with ratios and with chemical symbols.*

>   *Examples:*
>
>   The Babinski's reflex was **2+/3+** bilaterally.
>
>   The value was **-6.**
>
>   Titers of **1:80** or greater can be significant.
>
>   The CO_2 value was greater than the H_2O value.

14-M   *Use figures with blood pressure and temperature values.*

>   *Examples:*
>
>   His blood pressure was elevated at **160/90.**
>
>   A temperature of **99** degrees Fahrenheit or greater would be found in a febrile patient.

14-N   *Use figures with most drug values, but spell out the numbers when using words to describe frequency of a dosage less than 10. Be consistent in using either figures or spelling out numbers.*

>   *Examples:*
>
>   The patient was given **25 mEq** of Micro-K and prednisone **250 mg q.8h.** t.i.d. for **10 days.**
>
>   She was also given **1 inch** of Nitropaste every **four hours.**
>
>   He was to take the medication at a dosage of **400 mg one** every **12 hours** as needed.
>
>   Her mother was to take Dyazide **50 mg 2 capsules b.i.d. x 1 month.**

14-O   *With sutures, use figures including dashes and # signs.*

Examples:

The surgeon used **4-0** Prolene sutures.

The wound was repaired with **#1** nylon.

The pins were held in place with **#20 gauge** sutures.

14-P   *Use Roman numerals with cranial nerves, obstetrical history, electrocardiographic limb leads, types and factors, and cancer stages (see figure 22 for use of Roman numerals).*

Examples:

Cranial nerves **II through XII** were intact, although cranial nerve **VIII** showed minor abnormal signs.

She was **gravida III para II SAB I**.

Limb leads **II through V** on the EKG were misplaced.

The patient, who had **type II** hyperlipidemia, had a **factor VIII** drawn.

The carcinoma was **stage II**.

14-Q   *Use Arabic numerals with vertebrae and disc spaces, cardiac murmur grades, electrocardiographic chest leads, cancer grades and visual acuity.*

Examples:

There was a herniation at the **L5-S1** level, and a fracture at **C3**.

On cardiac examination, a grade **2/6** murmur was auscultated.

The sarcoma was **grade 2**.

Vision in the left eye was **20/400** and in the right eye was **20/60**.

14-R   *Use figures for Apgar ratings and spell out the minutes at which the test was done.*

Examples:

Although the infant was premature, Apgars were **6 and 8** at **one and five minutes**.

The baby had an initial Apgar score of **1** for heart rate, **1** for respiratory effort, **2** for muscle tone, **2** for reflex response and **1** for color.

FIGURE 22 Roman Numerals

Arabic Numeral	Roman Numeral
1	I
2	II
3	III
4	IV
5	V
6	VI
7	VII
8	VIII
9	IX
10	X
11	XI
12	XII
13	XIII
14	XIV
15	XV
16	XVI
17	XVII
18	XVIII
19	XIX
20	XX
30	XXX
40	XL
50	L
60	LX
70	LXX
80	LXXX
90	XC
100	C
200	CC
300	CCC
400	CD
500	D
600	DC
700	DCC
800	DCCC
900	CM
1000	M

14-S   *Spell out single-digit ordinals (numerals ending in -st, -nd, -rd, and -th) and use figures for double-digit ordinals. Use Roman numerals with ordinals if the number ordinarily takes a Roman numeral.*

Examples:

There were fractures of the **fourth, fifth** and **sixth** ribs.

The patient was in the **12th** grade.

The **VIIIth** cranial nerve was suspicious for nystagmus.

14-T   *Use figures and commas when expressing the day and the year in dates; usually write out the name of the month. Do not use commas when expressing only the month and year. Use ordinals only when the day precedes the month.*

Examples:

The patient's birthdate was **March 21, 1977**.

The operation was performed in **May 1965**, according to the patient.

She was admitted on the **12th of June**, and she was discharged on **July 29**.

14-U   *Use figures, a colon and a.m. or p.m. with standard units of time; use figures and the word "hours" with military units of time; and use figures and o'clock with positions of a clock to indicate direction or proximity to the poles (see Figure 23 for military time conversion).*

Examples:

The operation was performed at **8:00 a.m**.

She was brought to the emergency room at **1400 hours** yesterday.

An incision was made at the **9 o'clock** position.

14-V   *Use figures to indicate more than one item in a series in the following manner:*

Examples:

DISCHARGE DIAGNOSES:

      1.   Left lower lobe infiltrate.

      2.   Pneumonia.

 3. Hypertension.

 or. . .

OPERATIONS PERFORMED:

 1. Lumbar diskectomy.

 2. Decompression of cervical disc space #4.

 or...

The patient's case made the following impressions: 1) cervicodorsal strain; 2) cervicodorsal spasms; and 3) radiculitis, right arm.

 or...

ADMITTING DIAGNOSIS: Pleurisy and pulmonary edema.

FIGURE 23   Military Time Conversion Chart

Standard Time	Military Time
12:00 a.m. (midnight, begining of day)	0000 hours
1:00 a.m.	0100 hours
2:00 a.m.	0200 hours
3:00 a.m	0300 hours
4.00 a.m	0400 hours
5:00 a.m	0500 hours
6:00 a.m	0600 hours
7:00 a.m	0700 hours
8:00 a.m	0800 hours
9:00 a.m	0900 hours
10:00 a.m	1000 hours
11:00 a.m	1100 hours
12:00 p.m (noon)	1200 hours
1:00 p.m	1300 hours
2:00 p.m	1400 hours
3:00 p.m	1500 hours
4:00 p.m	1600 hours
5:00 p.m	1700 hours
6:00 p.m	1800 hours
7:00 p.m	1900 hours
8:00 p.m	2000 hours
9:00 p.m	2100 hours
10:00 p.m	2200 hours
11:00 p.m	2300 hours
12:00 p.m (midnight, end of day).	2400 hours

Unit 15

Commonly Confused Words, Misspelled Words and Spelling Hints

Overview: English can be a very difficult language to master. Many errors in writing are related to spelling. As a medical transcriptionist, you will find that many words are often confused or misspelled. To maintain your employer's or client's quality standards, you will have to be certain that the words you use are the correct words. Confused words can be a special problem, as most spell checking functions on word processing programs will not alert you to a confused word. Misspelled words will be flagged, but if the word is an acceptable word, incorrectly used or not, it will usually go unnoticed until printed or proofread (or in the worst case scenario, sent to the employer or client) unless you are familiar with commonly confused words. Constant consultation with a dictionary will provide the greatest help, although many spelling problems can be avoided by following a few rules. The following is a guide for spelling hints, commonly confused words and misspelled words.

15-A   Commonly Confused Words

The following words are often confused. Learn the differences in their meaning and spelling, so that when you encounter them in dictation you will be prepared to make the correct choice.

abduct (to flex away) vs. **adduct** (to flex inward)

accept (to receive willingly) vs. **except** (excluding)

advice (n. an opinion) vs. **advise** (v. to give an opinion)

a febrile patient (a patient with fever) vs. **an afebrile patient** (a patient without fever)

affect (n. psychological disposition) vs. **effect** (n. a result; or v. to cause or bring about change)

allusion (indirect or casual mention) vs. **elusion** (an evading of something) vs. **illusion** (misleading appearance)

anonymous (nameless or unidentified) vs. **unanimous** (unified, especially a vote)

ante- (before) vs. **anti-** (against)

anterior (pertaining to the front part) vs. **interior** (pertaining to the inside part) vs. **inferior** (pertaining to the lesser part)

arrhythmia (irregular heart rhythm) vs. **erythema** (redness, especially of the skin)

assure (to promise) vs. **ensure** (to guarantee) vs. **insure** (to provide insurance)

aural (pertaining to the ears) vs. **oral** (pertaining to the mouth)

carotene (a yellowish chemical pigment) vs. **keratin** (a protein found in teeth, skin and nails)

cella (an enclosure) vs. **sella** (a saddle)

censor (to edit) vs. **censure** (to reprimand)

cite (a notation) vs. **site** (location) vs. **sight** (vision)

climatic (pertaining to the weather) vs. **climactic** (pertaining to a climax)

coarse (thick) vs. **course** (a path or regimen)

complement (something that completes) vs. **compliment** (something that flatters or praises)

conscience (sense of moral standards, or sense of right and wrong) vs. **conscious** (state of being awake or alert)

cord (a thick string, such as the spinal cord) vs. **chord** (a string or group of strings that produces sound, such as a piano chords)

decision (a choice) vs. **discission** (an incision)

defuse (to strain or make nonfunctional) vs. **diffuse** (spread out)

descent (going down) vs. **dissent** (to disagree)

discreet (careful or prudent) vs. **discrete** (unrelated)

ductal (pertaining to a channel) vs. **ductile** (flexible)

dysphagia (inability to eat or swallow) vs. **dysphasia** (inability to speak)

effected (produced a desired result) vs. **affected** (influenced or emotionally moved)

elicit (bring forth) vs. **illicit** (unlawful)

emanate (come from) vs. **eminent** (prominent) vs. **imminent** (likely to happen)

enervation (weakening) vs. **innervation** (distribution of nerves) vs. **innovation** (new method)

explicit (distinct or not vague) vs. **implicit** (implied)

facial (having to do with the face) vs. **fascial** (having to do with fibrous tissue)

farther (an extra distance) vs. **further** (an additional amount; also)

Feldene (anti-arthritic medication) vs. **Seldane** (antihistamine medication)

flanges (dental edges or borders) vs. **phalanges** (fingers, toes or digital protrusion)

gauge (a measurement) vs. **gouge** (to scoop out)

idle (not active) vs. **idol** (symbol of worship)

ileum (intestine) vs. **ilium** (hip bone)

inter- (between) vs. **intra-** (within)

it's (contraction for it + is) vs. **its** (possessive pronoun for something belonging to it)

knuckle (dorsal aspect of the phalangeal joints) vs. **nuchal** (pertaining to the neck)

later (at a subsequent time) vs. **latter** (the second or more recent of two previously named items)

lay (to place or put — used with objects) vs. **lie** (to recline — used with subjects; to deceive)

led (past tense of the verb, to lead) vs. **lead** (present tense of the verb, to lead, or a chemical element)

liable (accountable) vs. **libel** (disparaging or defamatory comment)

lichen (plant formed from algae and fungus) vs. **liken** (to compare)

loop (a bend in a cordlike structure) vs. **loupe** (a magnifying lens)

loose (not tight) vs. **lose** (to misplace; to be defeated)

meiosis (cell division) vs. **miosis** (constriction of the pupils)

moral (a. ethical; n. lesson) vs. **morale** (attitude or mood)

mucous (adj. pertaining to mucus) vs. **mucus** (noun form of mucus)

osteal (bony) vs. **ostial** (pertaining to an opening into a tubular organ or between two body cavities)

packed (bundled) vs. **pact** (agreement)

palpation (examination by feeling with fingers) vs. **palpitation** (throbbing or arrhythmia)

paracytic (lying among cells) vs. **parasitic** (pertaining to a parasite)

passed (went by, dissipated or cessation) vs. **past** (in a former time)

pediculous (lice-infested) vs. **pediculus** (a pedicle or stemlike structure)

perfusion (a pouring through) vs. **profusion** (an abundance)

perineal (pertaining to the pelvic floor) vs. **perennial** (lasting a year or two years) vs. **peritoneal** (pertaining to the serous membrane lining the abdominopelvic walls) vs. **peroneal** (pertaining to the outer side of the leg)

petal (leaflike part) vs. **pedal** (pertaining to the foot)

plain (simple or single) vs. **plane** (a flat surface or a three-dimensional object)

precede (come before) vs. **proceed** (follow, or funds from an event)

principal (primary or head) vs. **principle** (a rule or law)

prostate (gland at the base of the male bladder) vs. **prostrate** (to lie flat; to overcome)

pupal (pertaining to the second stage of an insect) vs. **pupil** (pertaining to the eye)

radical (extreme) vs. **radicle** (a small root)

rational (reasonable or logical) vs. **rationale** (explanation or justification)

reflex (involuntary reaction) vs. **reflux** (backward or return flow)

regimen (any methodical system, such as diet or exercise) vs. **regiment** (section of an Army division or control with strict discipline) vs. **regime** (political or ruling system)

retrocolic (pertaining to the colon) vs. **retrocollic** (pertaining to the back of the neck)

right (n. direction opposite of left, a privilege; v. or adj. correct) vs. **write** (to compose or record)

root (embedded part, or cause) vs. **route** (path)

sac (pouchlike part) vs. **sack** (bag)

saccharin (a calorie-free sweetener) vs. **saccharine** (pertaining to sugar)

sail (v. to navigate; n. an object used to control wind on a boat) vs. **sale** (n. the selling of goods)

scatoma (fecal matter in the colon) vs. **scotoma** (area of depressed vision in the visual field)

scirrhous (hard) vs. **scirrhus** (a carcinoma)

set (to place something somewhere - used with objects) vs. **sit** (to rest on the buttocks — used with subjects; to remain for a time)

sitology (the study of dietetics) vs. **cytology** (cell biology)

stationary (immovable) vs. **stationery** (writing paper)

sycosis (hair follicle inflammation) vs. **psychosis** (mental disorder)

their (possessive pronoun meaning belonging to them) vs. **there** (a place not here) vs. **they're** (contraction for they + are)

to (prep. indicates movement toward) vs. **too** (adv. also) vs. **two** (a number following or greater than one)

-trophic (relating to nutrition) vs. **-tropic** (denoting a change)

vesical (pertaining to the bladder) vs. **vesicle** (a small sac containing liquid, especially of the skin)

viscous (having a high degree of friction when rubbed; thick and syrupy) vs. **viscus** (any of the large organs of the abdominal cavity)

waive (to defer or relinquish) vs. **wave** (v. to swell; n. a hand greeting)

who's (a contraction for who + is) vs. **whose** (a possessive form of the pronoun who)

Xanax (a tranquilizing medication) vs. **Zantac** (a medication for the treatment of ulcers)

your (possessive form of the pronoun you) vs. **you're** (contraction for you + are) vs. **yore** (long ago)

15-B   Commonly Misspelled Words

1.   Learn the correct spellings of these commonly misspelled English words:

absence	acknowledgment	acquaint
amateur	analyze	anonymous
apologize	approximately	argument
athletic	auxiliary	bankruptcy
brochure	calendar	category
commitment	committee	concede

congratulations	conscientious	consensus
copyright	criticism	criticize
embarrass	environment	equipped
exaggeration	explanation	familial
fascinate	February	fluctuate
foreign	foresee	fourth
fulfillment	grammar	incidentally
height	incidentally	insistence
integration	itinerary	judgment
leisure	liaison	license
likelihood	livelihood	loneliness
maintenance	miniaturc	miscellaneous
mortgage	necessary	ninety
noticeable	occurred	parallel
possession	privilege	profited
quandary	quantity	questionnaire
receipt	receive	recommendation
referral	relevant	restaurant
sacrilegious	schedule	separate
similar	sufficient	superintendent
supersede	supposedly	transferred
unanimous	undoubtedly	utilization

2. Learn the correct spellings of these commonly misspelled medical words:

accommodation	aggravated	alveolar
anthelix	anulus	apparent
aphthous	apneic	appendiceal
ascites	asymmetrical	asymptomatic
auricle	auricular	auscultation
breathe	bruit	buccal

caudal	choana	cholesteatoma
claudication	commissure	compatible
condyle	curette	curvilinear
defervescence	deglutition	dependent
desiccated	diarrhea	diuresis
Dyazide	ecchymosis	emittance
emphysema	empiric	eosinophil
erythema	Escherichia	eschar
exquisite	extraocular	fascicular
fluctuance	fluorescent	funduscopic
gallop	guaiac	hemoptysis
hyoid	inguinal	intermittent
in situ	in toto	Kerley B lines
labyrinthine	laryngeal	lysis
malar	maneuver	meconium
mucus	normocephalic	nystagmus
ophthalmology	palpitation	paresis
paroxysmal	phlegm	phonate
piriform sinus	Pseudomonas	pterygium
purulent	rhabdomyosarcoma	rhinitis
rhythm	sequelae	serpiginous
sialadenitis	Sjogrin's disease	sphenoid
tenacious	telangiectasia	threshold
tic	tinnitus	vesicular

15-C   Guidelines for Preferred Usage

It is acceptable to use some English words and word groups in a variety of ways. However, some words and word groups used frequently in medical dictation have preferred forms. Be sure to consult with the physician or facility for which you are transcribing before making extensive changes. The following is a list of some preferred forms of common phrases used in dictation:

Word/Word Group	Preferred Form
at all times	always
at the present time	now
at this point in time	now
be sure and	be sure to
could of	could have
due to the fact that	because, due to
for the purpose of	for
in order to	to
in regard to, in regards to, with regard to	regarding
in the event that	if, should
might of	might have
O.K., o.k.	okay
should of	should have
towards	toward
try and	try to
until such time as	until
would of	would have

15-D   Spelling Hints

1. **Do not rely exclusively on pronunciation.** With the English language, pronunciation of words is often an unreliable method of determining their spelling. For example, if a word ends in a sound similar to "uff", there could in fact be different correct suffixes, depending upon the word: **stuff** or **rough**. Also, words that look alike may not sound alike: **rough**, **through**, **dough** and **trough**.

2. **Do remember that there can be different forms of the same word.** Remember that homonyms are words that sound or are spelled alike but are different in meaning, and synonyms are words with the same meanings. If you are confused about the correct use or spelling of a word, consult a dictionary.

3. **Do use preferred, American spellings.** For example, use color instead of colour, theater instead of theatre, canceled instead of cancelled. Other

spellings (British, for example) usually use additional letters and often can confuse someone who has difficulty with spelling techniques.

4. **Do know the difference between words with "ie" and "ei" spellings.** Words such as receive and relieve sound alike, but the i + e combination is spelled differently in each. Use this clue to aid in spelling: "'I' before 'e', except after 'c', or when pronounced 'ay' as in **neighbor** and **weigh**."

    Examples:

    believe

    retrieve

    conceive

    freight

    Special note: There are several exceptions to the above clue. If you question a particular spelling with "ei" and "ie" combinations, consult a dictionary. Learn these major exceptions to the clue:

apartheid	being	caffeine	codeine
deity	either	Fahrenheit	feisty
fluorescein	foreign	forfeit	geiger
height	heifer	heir	heist
leisure	neither	protein	reveille
seismograph	seizure	sheik	Sheila
sleight of hand	sovereign	stein	weird

5. **Do know when to keep or drop the final "e".** Drop the e before adding **-able**, **-ible** or **-ing** if the ending begins with a vowel.

    Examples:

    advisable

    forcible

    surmising

    Exception: The silent e is kept to avoid confusion with another word, to avoid mispronunciation or after a soft **c** or **g**, to keep the sound of the consonant soft.

    Examples:

    dying v. dyeing [avoids confusion]

    singing v. singeing

    noticeable

6. **Do know when to keep or drop the final "y".** Change the y to i when it follows a consonant when adding an ending.

Examples:

hurry → hurries

apply → applied

7. **Do double consonants when adding an ending in single syllable words.** When a word has a single syllable, double the last consonant before adding the ending.

Examples:

stop → stopping

tan → tanned

Exceptions:

a. Do not usually double the final consonant when two vowels or a vowel and another consonant precede the final consonant.

   Examples:

   start → starting

   jump → jumped

b. Do double the final consonant when a single vowel precedes the final consonant and the stress falls on the last syllable of a two-syllable or more word.

   Examples:

   refer → referral

   begin → beginning

c. However, do not double the final consonant when two vowels or a vowel and another consonant precede the final consonant, or when the stress falls on a syllable other than the last syllable in a two-syllable or more word.

   Examples:

   refer → referendum

   resent → resentment

Unit 16

Editing Rules for the Medical Transcriptionist

Overview: As stated in Unit 1, a successful and proficient medical transcriptionist must know when, as well as how, to edit. What is editing? Editing is the process of integrating word usage, grammar, punctuation, correct spelling and other mechanics into dictation to make the transcription clear, concise and logical. Transcriptionists must use any prescribed guidelines given by the dictator or employer as well as their own discretion regarding the proper place, time and manner in which to edit dictation. The following is a brief editing guide.

16-A   When to Edit

1.   Edit dictation when it is grammatically incorrect.

Examples:

Dictation: "Her mother and her are to follow up with either Dr. Smith or I in two days."

Transcription: Her mother and she are to follow up with either Dr. Smith or me in two days.
      ("Her" is an objective pronoun. "She" should be used because the pronoun is part of the subject of the sentence. Also, the preposition "with" takes an objective pronoun "me", instead of the subjective pronoun "I".)

Dictation: "The disease which the patient had he was treated for."

Transcription: The patient was treated for the disease that he had.
      (The word "which" introduces a nonrestrictive clause, while "that" introduces a restrictive clause, and the sentence contains a restrictive clause, as it cannot be removed and have the same meaning. Also, the sentence ends in a preposition, so the sentence should be rearranged so it will not end in a preposition.)

Dictation: "There was no hemorrhages, exudates or erythema on exam."

Transcription: There were no hemorrhages, exudates or erythema on exam.

("There was" should be used with singular objects. "There were" should be used with plural objects, or a combination of plural and singular objects.)

2. Edit dictation when it is unclear, ambiguous, or could result in misreading or misunderstanding.

Examples:

Dictation: "The patient had mild obstruction sitting in the chair."

Transcription: The patient had mild obstruction, while sitting in the chair.
   (The dictated sentence implies that the patient's obstruction was actually sitting in the chair. The transcribed sentence clarifies that the mild obstruction occurred while the patient was sitting in the chair.)

Dictation: "I will see her back in two days for re-exam."

Transcription: I will see her again in two days for re-examination.

or

She will come back to the office in two days for reexamination.
   (The dictated sentence is ambiguous, implying that the dictator will be examining the patient's spine, or back, in two days. The transcribed sentence clarifies the fact that the patient will be seen and re-examined again in two days. The dictation actually was dictated by an otolaryngologist, who would not typically be examining the patient's back or spine.)

Dictation: "Dr. Brown, the patient's primary care physician, was contacted after he had the myocardial infarction."

Transcription: Dr. Brown, the patient's primary care physician, was contacted after the patient had the myocardial infarction.
   (The dictated sentence implies that Dr. Brown, the physician, had the myocardial infarction. In fact, from the context of the dictation, the patient had actually had the heart attack. The transcribed sentence makes the sentence clearer.)

3. Edit dictation when there is a medical or logical inconsistency.

Examples:

Dictation: "The hemoglobin was 42.7 and the hematocrit was 14.1."

Transcription: The hemoglobin was 14.1 and the hematocrit was 42.7.
   (The normal reference value range for hemoglobin is from 12–18 grams, and the normal reference value range for hematocrit is 37–52% [See Appendix D]. Although laboratory results are often well outside the

normal reference value range, it seems obvious that the dictator has transposed the values, which has resulted in a medical inconsistency and should be changed or flagged ["flagging" a report is attaching a sticky-backed note or a colored tag to the printed report]. If you were unsure as to whether or not the dictation should remain as stated, print out a copy of both transcribed reports, as directed in section 16-C #3, below.)

Dictation: "The cardiologist was consulted, as the patient had marked erythema on his EKG."

Transcription: The cardiologist was consulted, as the patient had marked arrhythmia on his EKG.

("Erythema" means redness or flushing of the skin or membrane. "Arrhythmia" means a variation from the normal rhythm of the heart beat. An electrocardiogram measures electrical currents of the heart; therefore, the use of the word "erythema" would be a medical inconsistency, as erythema could not be measured or detected on an electrocardiogram. Again, if you are unsure as to whether or not the dictation should be edited, print two copies, as directed in section 16-C #3, below.)

Dictation: "The patient was seen in December of this year."

Transcribed: The patient was seen in December of 1990.

(The above dictation was done in March of 1991. Since December of 1991 had not yet come when the dictation was dictated, it is illogical and incorrect to transcribe that the patient was seen in the future, as was dictated. The transcription should be changed to reflect what the dictator apparently intended to say. If you were uncertain as to the year, yet you knew that what was dictated was incorrect, again, you could print out two copies of the transcribed report, as directed in section 16-C #3, below.)

16-B   When Not to Edit

1.   Do not edit dictation when there is an inconsistency that you are unsure about or when you are not reasonably sure about how to make a correction.

Examples:

Dictation: "She had thrombophlebitis of the left leg. . . .ASSESSMENT: Thrombophlebitis, right leg."

Transcription: She had thrombophlebitis of the _____ leg. . . .ASSESSMENT: Thrombophlebitis, _____ leg.

(It is unclear to which leg the dictator is referring, as the dictation mentions first the left leg, and then, later on, the right leg. Since it is not possible for us to know with certainty which leg is the correct one, we should leave a blank and attach a note describing the problem in the dictation.)

Dictation: "PERRL. The left pupil was slightly unreactive."

Transcription: [Same.]
(This transcription should be flagged, but left as is. It seems to be inconsistent that the left eye could be both reactive [PERRL = pupils equal, round and reactive to light] and at the same time slightly unreactive. However, you cannot be sure as to how to edit the dictation, so you should leave it as is and point out the inconsistency to the dictator.)

Dictation: "The patient had a mucousy discharge."

Transcription: [Same.]
(Although the spell checking function on the word processor identifies the word "mucousy" as being an unacceptable word, and upon looking up the word in the dictionary no listing can be found, the dictation should remain as is, as there is no acceptable way to correct the word without making a slight change in the meaning of the sentence.)

2.   Do not edit dictation if you are unsure of the dictator's meaning.

Examples:

Dictation: "The patient had PE on exam of the chest and lungs."

Transcription: [Same.]
(This transcription should be flagged, but left as is. You cannot be sure to which abbreviation the dictator is referring, as "PE" could stand for pulmonary edema, pleural effusion, or pulmonary embolism, all of which would be appropriate in an examination of the chest and lungs. Since you cannot be sure as to the correct abbreviation, you should leave it as is and point out the fact that the abbreviation remains in the transcription to the dictator.)

Dictation: "He was a 25 pack-a-day smoker."

Transcription: Hc was a _____ pack-a-day smoker.
(In this dictation, "25 pack-a-day" smoker seems to be a logical inconsistency. You cannot be sure, however, whether the dictator means the subject smoked 25 cigarettes a day or something else. Therefore, a blank should be left and the transcription should be flagged.)

Dictation: "A chest x-ray was within. . .(cut-off). . .limits."

Transcription: A chest x-ray was within _____ limits.
(You might assume that the dictator means to say "normal" where he is cut off, but you cannot be sure. Therefore, you should leave a blank and flag the transcription.)

3.   Do not edit dictation if the editing changes would alter the dictator's meaning or style.

Examples:

Dictation: "Chest and lungs clear. No obvious changes since last exam. Will see patient back two days postop."

Transcription: [Same.]

(Changing the dictated sentence grammatically by inserting articles, subjects and predicates would result in changing the dictator's style.)

Dictation: "By her history, the patient had been afflicted with depression throughout the majority of her life. With regard to her status of mental condition on examination, she was at all times lucid in processes of thought and speech. She was admitted due to the fact that observation was a necessary requirement until such time as she was felt to be of little danger to herself."

Transcription: [Same.]

(Although this dictation is obviously wordy and contains several examples of word groups that should be replaced with preferred forms [see Unit 15], this type of dictation seems to be the dictator's personal style. Since changing every instance of wordiness in transcribing this report could result in altering the dictator's style or meaning, you should not edit this type of dictation without prior discussion with the dictator or approval by a supervisor.)

Dictation: She will follow up with her primary care and myself in two weeks.

Transcription: [Same.]

(There are two instances of individual style in this dictated sentence. The first, "her primary care" probably refers to her primary care physician, but this dictator's style is to leave out the word "physician", so you should leave the dictation as is. After consultation with the individual dictator, he or she may allow you to alter the transcription to contain the ·word "physician", but do not alter dictation such as this without prior approval by the dictator. Also, it is preferable to use the objective pronoun "me" at the end of the sentence instead of the reflexive pronoun "myself", but this dictator's style is to use reflexive pronouns in this case to sound more formal. Again, do not alter this type of dictation without prior approval or discussion.)

16-C   Special Notes

1.   Always take into consideration physicians', hospitals' or clients' policies and preferences when there is a question of whether or not to edit.

2.   Always be prepared to support your editing changes. When there might be some question about something you have edited, or the manner in which you have edited, supply copies of written documentation from the reference materials or sources you used in making the editing changes.

3.   If you are unsure as to whether the physician or dictator would approve of an edit, enclose printed copies of both the transcription the way it was originally dictated as well as the edited version of the transcription. Make a notation on an attached separate piece of paper of where and why you made the edit.

4.   Remember that certain dictators have specific individual styles, and the dictator likely does not want his or her personal style altered by a transcriptionist. If a physician, for instance, consistently dictates in sentence fragments, and this is obviously the physician's style, do not correct the sentences by making them complete. Leave the transcription as dictated; if the physician wants corrections, the document will be sent back with specified revisions.

5.   Do not edit to reflect your own personal writing style. You are not the author of your transcription; you are simply the one who transforms spoken language into written language. Only edit for reasons explained in section 16-A.

6.   Always leave a blank in the transcription if you cannot understand or hear some part of a dictation, if you feel there is an error or inconsistency that you cannot correct, of if the dictator is cut off in his or her dictation. Always make a notation on a separate piece of paper informing the dictator that you have, indeed, left a blank.

7.   Always double check a dictator's spelling. Though it is out of consideration for the transcriptionist that the dictator usually goes to the trouble of spelling out a word, many times the spelling is nevertheless incorrect. Always look up unfamiliar words and spellings.

8.   Always keep in mind that as all people differ, so do dictators. While some dictators may appreciate frequent and thorough editing, others may regard the dictation as being "their creation" and may resent such intervention, no matter how admirable the intentions of the transcriptionist. Be prepared to work with such dictators, and realize that the dictators are ultimately responsible for the content of the report, as their signatures affirm its quality, authenticity and accuracy. Remember that the role of the medical transcriptionist is to help transform the transcription into clear, concise and more logical expressions of the same information, without reflecting the personal style, views or attitude of the transcriptionist.

16-D   Humor versus Respect in Editing

All medical transcriptionists are likely to encounter, at some time during their careers, a dictated or transcribed word, phrase or sentence that strikes them as being humorous or amusing. It is natural to chuckle in these instances and you may feel free to do so; always keep in mind, however, that the transcription of medical records is serious business, and the confidentiality, sensitivity and privacy of the patient and dictator must always be maintained. Here are a few examples of some phrases the author has encountered in proofreading transcribed dictation that hopefully will provide you with some amusement and help you to realize that medical transcription is not only a somber profession, but at times can also provide a source of comical diversion.

1.   Transcribed: "She would be a candidate for hearing aids if she sewed the sides."

   (The transcriptionist misheard "sewed the sides," when in fact the dictator meant "so decides.")

2.   Transcribed: "The patient had no stupus."

   (The transcriptionist misheard a nonexistent word "stupus"; the dictator actually said "stiffness".)

3.   Transcribed: "I will be in contact with the patient following his road testing."

   (The transcriptionist mistook the words "his road testing" for simply "further nose testing.")

4.   Transcribed: "The youngster still has food in his ears."

   (The transcriptionist mistook the word "food" for "fluid.")

5.   Transcribed: "The patient complained of a beasting."

   (After listening to the tape, and spending several minutes consulting a dictionary in an attempt to find an entry for "beasting", it was discovered that the dictator had actually said "bee sting.")

Unit Applications

The unit applications, or activities, that follow are designed as a supplemental study aid to the handbook portion of this text. The activities are designed to help you further understand the history, environment, tools, formats and mechanics used in transcribing medical records. There are two types of exercise activities: review exercises and revision exercises. In the review exercises your goal is to furnish correct answers to specific questions asked regarding material in the text of each unit. In the revision exercises your objective is to proofread, correct and transcribe into typewritten or word processed form a portion of text in which you will use the overall concepts you have learned so far. Consult with your instructor about how and when to complete and submit the exercises.

Unit 1: What Is Medical Transcription?

Review Exercises

Short Answers

1. Describe the first historical form of medical documentation.

   _____

   _____

   _____

2. Who was Hippocrates, and how was he important in the development of medical documentation?

   _____

   _____

   _____

3. What sentence in the Hippocratic Oath refers to confidentiality in medical records information?

   _____

   _____

   _____

4. List the requirements for a successful medical transcriptionist, and the skills needed.

   _____

   _____

   _____

5. What is editing? Describe how editing transforms dictation.

   _____

   _____

   _____

6. What basic equipment should a medical transcriptionist have at the work station?

   _____

   _____

   _____

7. What are the three basic parts of the audiocassette voice transcriber?

_____

_____

_____

8. List the three controls found on the transcriber's footpedal, and the three controls found on the transcriber's base that a transcriptionist can adjust to fit his or her own needs.

_____

_____

_____

9. Briefly describe the differences between the three types of audiocassette transcriber.

_____

_____

_____

10. List the three major medical transcription environments. Name the environment in which the medical transcriptionist has the most contact with the physician/dictator.

_____

_____

_____

True or False

1. T F   A medical transcriptionist and a medical transcriber is one in the same.
2. T F   The Hippocratic Oath instructs those practicing in the medical field to refrain from divulging work-related information.
3. T F   Medical transcriptionists are part translator, part transcriber, part nurse and part editor.
4. T F   Medical records can be subpoenaed and used as legal documentation in a court of law.
5. T F   Medical transcriptionists should be familiar with etymology—the study of word origins.
6. T F   The greatest tool a medical transcriptionist has at his or her fingertips is the word processor.

7. T F The physician is always available to directly answer a medical transcriptionist's questions.

8. T F On most transcribers, the play pedal is located on the left side of the transcriber's footpedal.

9. T F It is not always necessary to contact your supervisor before speaking with a dictating physician.

10. T F Mini-cassette tapes can usually be purchased in supermarkets and department stores.

Unit 2: Microcomputer Tools:
An Introduction to Word Processing

Review Exercises

Short Answers

1. Define "word processing."

   _____

   _____

   _____

2. Define "microcomputer."

   _____

   _____

   _____

3. What is a word processing program? Give an example of a specific word processing program.

   _____

   _____

   _____

4. What are the four major parts (hardware) of the microcomputer?

   _____

   _____

   _____

5. Describe at least three features of the central processing unit (CPU).

   _____

   _____

   _____

6. What is microcomputer software?

   _____

   _____

   _____

7. Briefly explain bytes, kilobytes and megabytes, and how they relate to the microcomputer's memory.

    _____

    _____

    _____

8. Briefly explain what formatting does to a diskette.

    _____

    _____

    _____

9. What is a hard disk drive?

    _____

    _____

    _____

10. Give three rules for diskette handling.

    _____

    _____

    _____

Fill in the Blanks

1. The monitor is the component of the computer that is also known as the

    _____.

2. The _____ key is a special key that allows you to place new characters into existing text without replacing the old ones.

3. The process of turning on the central processing unit's power supply and getting to the prompt on the microcomputer's monitor is called _____.

4. A daisywheel printer is a _____ quality printer.

5. A data storage capacity of 360,000 bytes would be found on a _____ - inch floppy diskette.

6. Similar to a file drawer in a file cabinet, a _____ can help you organize your disk filing system.

7. All blank diskettes need to be _____ before being used.

8. A hard drive may be divided into parts, called _____.

9. When handling a diskette, be sure to touch only the top of the diskette, near the _____.

10. Exposure to dust, liquids or magnetized devices could alter the _____ _____ impressions of the mylar diskette.

Unit 3: Use of Reference Materials

Review Exercises

Short Answers

1. Describe how to use the *Physician's Desk Reference.*

   _____

   _____

   _____

2. Explain the difference between the PDR and a drug index/catalogue.

   _____

   _____

   _____

3. What types of references can be used to locate misspelled or misused words?

   _____

   _____

   _____

4. Explain the difference between a medical dictionary and a medical word book.

   _____

   _____

   _____

5. Describe the two types of medical word books.

   _____

   _____

   _____

6. What is a medical specialty word book?

   _____

   _____

   _____

7. For what purpose would you use a grammar reference book?

    _____

    _____

    _____

8. Why might a drug index be preferable to the *Physician's Desk Reference* for a
    medical transcriptionist?

    _____

    _____

    _____

9. The *Medical Phrase Index* falls into which category of reference materials?

    _____

    _____

    _____

10. In which reference material(s) would you be able to look up the spelling of the
    word "hysterectomy"?

    _____

    _____

    _____

Special Exercise

Look up the word "bronchodilator" in a medical dictionary, a word book, a *Physician's
Desk Reference*, and a drug index/catalogue. Describe the method you used to locate the
word, and then write a definition/summary of all information found under each entry.

_____

_____

_____

_____

_____

_____

_____

_____

Unit 4: Types of Medical Reports and Formats

Review Exercises

Short Answers

1. List the six types of medical reports.

   _____

   _____

   _____

2. Explain the focus of the history and physical report.

   _____

   _____

   _____

3. List six major parts (section headings) contained in the report describing an operative procedure.

   _____

   _____

   _____

4. Who dictates the consultation report, and who receives the report?

   _____

   _____

   _____

5. Explain the focus of the pathology report.

   _____

   _____

   _____

6. List three types of radiology diagnostic procedures.

   _____

   _____

   _____

7. List six section headings contained in the dismissal summary.

_____

_____

_____

8. What are "current" reports, and what is the usual turnaround time for these reports?

_____

_____

_____

9. Which reports are almost always dictated by someone other than the attending physician?

_____

_____

_____

10. Which type of report contains the heading "PROCEDURE"?

_____

_____

_____

Matching

Match each section heading in Column I with its associated report type in Column II. (Report types may be used more than once.)

COLUMN I

_____ 1. FLUOROSCOPIC CATHETERIZATION

_____ 2. HOSPITAL COURSE

_____ 3. REVIEW OF SYSTEMS

_____ 4. Sponge count

_____ 5. GROSS and MICROSCOPIC FINDINGS

_____ 6. RECOMMENDATIONS

COLUMN II

a. History and Physical Report

b. Operative Note

c. Consultation Report

d. Pathology Report

e. Radiology Report

f. Discharge Summary

_____   **7.** FOLLOW-UP

_____   **8.** TISSUE SUBMITTED

_____   **9.** CHIEF COMPLAINT

_____   **10.** FIRST ASSISTANT

Revision Exercise

Rekey the following history and physical report. In the revision, identify and label all unmarked section headings (e.g., **SUBJECTIVE:**, **OBJECTIVE:**, **Past History:**, **LABORATORY DATA:**, etc.) that are enclosed in parentheses. When you rekey the report, name the section headings without the parentheses, as in the format examples in Unit 4, Figures 8 through 15. Separate the two pages of the report in an appropriate manner.

```
          (section heading) Difficulty urinating.

          (section heading) The patient is a 45-year-old, white,
          married male who enters the hospital emergency room
          complaining of frequency, urgency and pain on urination.
          These symptoms were of sudden onset the night before
          admission at about 1:00 a.m. He noted a foul odor from his
          last urination, which was yesterday.

          (section heading) The patient had frequent urinary tract
          infections as a child. His childhood illnesses included
          chickenpox and measles. He had an appendectomy at age 15.

          (section heading) His father had a transurethral resection
          of the prostate at age 51, and he died at 62 of a testicular
          carcinoma.

          (section heading)
          Head, eyes, ears, nose and throat: Negative history.
          Cardiovascular: No chest pain. He has a history of
          hypertension.
          Gastrointestinal: Negative history.
          Genitourinary: Recent complaint of dysuria, as noted above.
          Extremities: Negative history.
          Neurologic: Negative history.




          CONTINUED

          JONATHAN SMITH, M.D.                BRANCH, ADAM #101010
          D&T:

          (NAME OF REPORT)
```

Page 2

(section heading)
Vital signs: Temperature 98.6, respiration rate 28, pulse
rate 80 and blood pressure 122/94. He weighs 185 pounds.
General: He is a well-developed, well-nourished, white male
in moderate distress.
Head: Normocephalic.
Eyes: Funduscopic exam is normal. No conjunctivitis. Slight
exophthalmos.
Ears: Tympanic membranes are normal. No acoustic deficits.
Nose: Normal septum. Evidence of recent epistaxis, with a
small amount of dried blood present.
Throat: No erythema or exudates. The tonsils are normal.
There is no hypopharyngeal swelling on palpation.
Cardiovascular: There is increased diastolic pressure, with
a blood pressure of 122/94.
Gastrointestinal: Soft, with active bowel sounds. Normal
rebound. No hepatosplenomegaly.
Genitourinary: Some tenderness in the groin and
suprapubically. No prostate swelling. Epididymis, testes,
symphysis pubis and urethral orifice all appear to be normal
by palpation.
Musculoskeletal: Upper and lower extremities negative.
Normal muscle tone and reflexes.
Neurologic: Negative.

(section heading)
1. Acute urinary tract infection, with polyuria, hematuria,
   proteinuria and bacteriuria.
2. Hypertension.
3. Incidental finding of status post epistaxis.

(section heading) We will give the patient Pyridium and
Bactrim DS b.i.d. We will send the patient home. He should
schedule an outpatient intravenous pyelogram within the next
week with his primary care physician.

JONATHAN SMITH, M.D.   BRANCH, ADAM #101010
D&T:

(NAME OF REPORT)

Unit 5:   Medical Office Charting and Correspondence

Review Exercises

Short Answers

1. Describe how hospital admissions and medical office visits differ.

   _____

   _____

   _____

2. What is the usual turnaround time for medical office charting?

   _____

   _____

   _____

3. List the three types of medical office visits and the corresponding chart notes.

   _____

   _____

   _____

4. Which type of chart note would contain a re-evaluation of the patient?

   _____

   _____

   _____

5. What are the two basic categories of privately practicing physicians, and how does their correspondence differ?

   _____

   _____

   _____

6. List the three types of medical office chart note formats.

   _____

   _____

   _____

7. What is the difference between objective and subjective data, and what are their equivalents in the "HPIP" format?

_____

_____

_____

8. List the three basic types of medical office correspondence (letter) styles.

_____

_____

_____

9. What is the difference between mixed and open punctuation?

_____

_____

_____

10. Which letter style contains a tab at the beginning of each new paragraph?

_____

_____

_____

True or False

1. T F One medical office visit can be linked to another office visit.
2. T F The work-up is made on three levels: the signs, the symptoms and the diagnosis.
3. T F Check-ups are usually performed on new patients.
4. T F Internists dictate letters of introduction.
5. T F A patient's signs are "subjective" findings and a patient's symptoms are "objective" findings.
6. T F The problem-oriented format is usually used for follow-ups.
7. T F With left justified letters, text is equally spaced between margins and lines up on both margins.
8. T F Many clinics and offices are switching from the photocopy (pc:) notation to the carbon copy (cc:) notation.
9. T F Try to avoid dividing the last word on a page, and also try to avoid widows and orphans.
10. T F The complimentary close and signature block should not stand alone on a page.

Revision Exercise

Rekey the following medical correspondence. Use the full block letter style for the first letter and the modified semi-block style for the second letter. Follow the formats given in Unit 5, Figures 18 through 20. The date of the dictation for the letters is 3/1/91. Both letters should be addressed to: John Jones, M.D., 800 Broadway, Parker, CA 90001. The patient's name for the first letter is Paula Peters. The patient's name for the second letter is Henry Hobbs. The dictating physician's name is Robert P. Rose, M.D. Copies need to be sent to Dr. Dick Doggett on the first letter, and to Dr. Bob Brady and Ms. Valerie Vallejos on the second letter. There are enclosures with the first letter.

```
Dear John:

Ms. Peters presents with a complaint of choking. She tells
me that she has had three episodes over the last 18 months
where she chokes and actually loses her airway. She also
tells me that she knows of nothing specific that brings on
these attacks and nothing that relieves them. In speaking
with her regarding her hypopharynx, she tells me that she
does have esophageal reflux.

Fiberoptic examination of the nose, oropharynx and
hypopharynx was not remarkable. Evaluation of the larynx was
not remarkable as well, with the exception of the
arytenoids. The arytenoids are mildly inflamed and engorged.
The general head and neck examination was unremarkable.

I suspect she may well have a small esophageal reflux that
is not showing up on x-ray. This, of course, would make her
larynx more susceptible to laryngospasm and may well be the
source of her problem. I have asked that she obtain all of
the records regarding the various x-rays of her esophagus
and larynx that you have obtained to help me with my
evaluation. At this time I am going to put her on an
anti-reflux regimen and have her call me in three weeks for
follow-up.

Thank you for your referral.

Sincerely,
```

Dear John:

Mr. Hobbs was in today for evaluation of his vertigo. By his history, he experiences true spinning vertigo that is both subjective and objective. When these episodes occur he notes a lack of balance with veering to the right and left. Occasionally he has headache with this, and he also has occasional nausea and vomiting. These problems first began at age 8 years and they lasted until he was 12. From age 12 to age 28 he was symptom-free, and he had this problem recur one year ago. He has had four episodes since that time. The episodes last from roughly two to four days. During the episode he notes that change in position will make him dizzy. He admits to problems with walking, as mentioned above. The diazepam you have prescribed has helped with his vertigo to a large extent. He does have occasional tinnitus involving the right, but during acute episodes he denies worsening or the onset of tinnitus. He complains of some mild hearing loss. He also complains of fullness in both ears during these episodes. He experiences a blue/green aura before the episodes and notes what he describes as movement of his vision, and I suspect that he is not describing double vision, but true nystagmus instead.

Evaluation of the ears, nose and throat was not remarkable. The cranial nerves II through XII were intact. The corneal reflexes were intact. There was a slight lateral gaze nystagmus. The Romberg, tandem gait and cerebellar examinations were also normal.

My impression at this time is Meniere's disease. We are going to proceed with a full workup of his disorder. Upon completion of this workup I will be back in touch with the test results.

Thank you, again, for referring this pleasant gentleman.

Sincerely,

Unit 6: Word Usage

Review Exercises

Short Answers

1. What are phonetics, and how can they help you spell a word?

   _____

   _____

   _____

2. What is etymology, and how can it help you break down and spell a word?

   _____

   _____

   _____

3. Briefly define and give two examples of acronyms.

   _____

   _____

   _____

4. Briefly define and give two examples of homonyms.

   _____

   _____

   _____

5. Briefly define and give two examples of synonyms.

   _____

   _____

   _____

6. Briefly define and give two examples of antonyms.

   _____

   _____

   _____

7. What can happen when an acronym becomes a common expression?

_____

_____

_____

8. What is the difference between a homonym and a synonym?

_____

_____

_____

9. Using etymology, what is the definition of the word "cystoscope"?

_____

_____

_____

10. Using etymology, what is the definition of the word "demyelinate"?

_____

_____

_____

Special Exercise

Using phonetic keys to pronunciation, spell the correct word dictated as follows: "NEE-mahs-THEE-nee-uh". Show your work.

_____

_____

_____

_____

_____

_____

_____

_____

Matching

Match each word in Column I with its etymological breakdown in Column II.

	COLUMN I	COLUMN II
_____	**1.** acoustic neuroma	a. whitish rottening of the skin
_____	**2.** bradytachycardia	b. development of a blood cell
_____	**3.** diskectomy	c. surgical connection of the uterus and fallopian tubes
_____	**4.** erythedema	
_____	**5.** keratocyte	d. alternating rapid and slow pulse
_____	**6.** leukonecrosis	e. breaking down of bone and cartilage
_____	**7.** pyretic	f. a tumor of the auditory nerve
_____	**8.** osteochondrolysis	g. reddening and swelling of the skin
_____	**9.** salpingo-uterostomy	h. a horn-shaped cell
_____	**10.** thrombogenesis	i. surgical removal of a vertebral disc
		j. relating to fever

Unit 7: Sentence Grammar

Review Exercises

Short Answers

1. List the six types of nouns. Give an example of each type of noun.

   _____

   _____

   _____

2. List the five types of pronouns. Give an example of each type of pronoun.

   _____

   _____

   _____

3. List the three cases of pronouns.

   _____

   _____

   _____

4. What is an indefinite pronoun? Give five examples of indefinite pronouns.

   _____

   _____

   _____

5. Name the indefinite pronouns that can take a plural verb.

   _____

   _____

   _____

6. List the five major verb forms. Give an example of each major form of the verb "drink".

   _____

   _____

   _____

7. List the suffixes that give you clues that a medical word is an adjective.

_____

_____

_____

8. What is the rule for using "that" and "which" with clauses?

_____

_____

_____

9. Name two of the rules for prepositions.

_____

_____

_____

10. What is the rule regarding the verb forms of "lie", "lay", "sit" and "set"?

_____

_____

_____

Fill in the Blanks

Fill in the blank spaces with the correct pronoun or verb contained in parentheses.

1. Everyone _____ a sigh of relief when a surgical procedure is finished. (breathe, breathes)

2. Either the nurse or the physician's assistant _____ patients consent forms. (give, gives)

3. Someone has _____ facts confused. (his, their)

4. Every obstetrician has _____ own way of counseling expectant parents. (his or her, their)

5. The medical school graduates composed _____ class song. (its, their)

6. Surely someone among all the expert surgeons _____ the answer. (know, knows)

7. Neither the nurse nor the midwife _____ the procedure. (prefer, prefers)

8.   None of the surgical instruments _____ on the cart. (was, were)

9.   All of the 50 otolaryngologists visited _____ patients biweekly. (his or her, their)

10. The new dentistry class had _____ own philosophy. (its, their)

Identification/Fill in the Blanks

1.   Identify the four underlined words in each sentence as either a subject (s.), verb (v.), direct object (d.o.) or indirect object (i.o.):

   a.   Hospitals provide the sick with care.

   _____ _____ _____ _____

   b.   The surgeon called the operation a success.

   _____ _____ _____ _____

2.   Identify the four underlined words in each sentence as either an adjective (adj.) or adverb (adv.):

   a.   The patient was an obese, diaphoretic male who spoke very euphorically.

   _____ _____ _____ _____

   b.   The catheter was clamped tightly, and there was no visible evidence of purulent or hematic drainage.

   _____ _____ _____ _____

3.   Fill in the blanks with a logical preposition:

   a.   The nurse put the specimen container _____ the shelf.

   b.   The patient who was standing _____ the room, saw the physician take the file folder _____ the counter _____ him.

4.   Pick the correct verb:

   a.   The medical assistant _____ the bandage on the table. (lied, laid)

   b.   Patients are to _____ in the waiting room. (sit, set)

   c.   The transcriptionist _____ charts on the left everyday. (sits, sets)

   d.   " _____ down," the osteopath yelled to the patient. (lie, lay)

Revision Exercise

Rekey the following report, using correct grammar and complete sentences containing subjects, predicates and articles whenever possible. Consult regular and medical dictionaries when necessary.

```
DATE OF CONSULTATION: 10/31/80

REASON FOR CONSULTATION: Acute hepatitis.

Thank you for letting Dr. Josephs and I see Mr. Brandon
Carlton, 35-year-old industrial painter, in consultation.
Entered on account of four days of nausea and vomiting,
inability to eat and dizziness getting out of bed. Him was
feeling well until Thanksgiving Day following which he
developed a respiratory infection. He then has chilly
sensations, fever, cough, nasal drainage and blood-stained
mucus down the nose and throat. He did not have no food
because he could not hold anything down. His appetite is
only moderate at this time and he think he lost 5 pounds of
weight. He then noted that his skin become yellowish and his
urine dark. He attributes his abdominal pain to eating out,
that he did at the "Roach Coach" three days ago.

On examination, the patient is laying down. He looks ill but
afebrile with jaundiced eyes and skin. Tongue is coated. The
chest and lungs sounds relatively clear. The heart enlarged
without gallop or murmur. A 3+ positive Murphy's sign are
present. Belly is scaphoid, with audible peristalsis and an
healed inguinal hernia scar. No testicular masses or
recurrent hernias was present. There is no signs of edema.

IMPRESSION: This syndrome is thought by me to most likely be
viral hepatitis. It is possible he has overdosed on Tylenol,
but I do not thinks so. From the history, alcoholic
hepatitis or biliary tract stones seems unlikely.

RECOMMENDATIONS: If I was to make a suggestion, I would say
that he needs intravenous fluids. Also, a look at his
biliary tract with ultrasound make sense. We should hold
solid food until us have further information about the
ultrasound test, in case he needs a endoscopic procedure.

Thank you very much for permitting Dr. Josephs and I to see
this patient, who I have developed a great relationship with.

RONALD PARKER, M.D.              CARLTON, BRANDON #101011
D&T:


(NAME OF REPORT)D
```

Unit 8: Punctuation

Review Exercises

Short Answers

1. Give two instances in which you should use a period.

    _____

    _____

    _____

2. Give three instances in which you should use a comma.

    _____

    _____

    _____

3. Give two instances in which you should use a colon.

    _____

    _____

    _____

4. Give two instances in which you should use a semicolon.

    _____

    _____

    _____

5. Give two instances in which you should use an apostrophe.

    _____

    _____

    _____

6. Give two instances in which you should use quotation marks.

    _____

    _____

    _____

7. Explain two differences between a dash and a hyphen.

_____

_____

_____

8. Explain the two uses of parentheses.

_____

_____

_____

9. Explain the uses of ellipses.

_____

_____

_____

10. Explain the uses of slashes.

_____

_____

_____

Revision Exercise

Rekey the following sentences, using proper punctuation and rewriting them when necessary.

1. The patient was advised of the operative risks and potential complications which included the following bleeding at 10 to 14 days or at 24 hours a perforation necessitating further surgery and facial numbness and tingling

2. Physical examination revealed a well developed well nourished slightly obese Caucasian female who had a temperature of 99.6 degrees Fahrenheit a pulse of 88 respirations of 24 and a blood pressure of 128/82

3. His fractured right foot was reduced and placed in a blue boot he was advised to get some crutches for ambulation

4. Follow up is to be with Dr. MacIntosh in two days and the patient is to have a visiting nurse come to his residence twice a week beginning Saturday

5. In order to ascertain his orientation the physician repetitively asked the patient Do you know where you are in a loud voice

6. When the physician saw that a sponge had been left in the wound overnight he ex-
    claimed We have quite a problem here

7. Confused about what the physician meant the transcriptionist left a blank however
    she also flagged the report which would indicate to medical records that there was
    a problem

8. The physicians notes were indecipherable because he never remembered to dot
    his is and cross his ts nonetheless he probably received all As in college

9. The ovoid cyanotic lesion not a good sign in a patient in this condition was
    biopsied

10. Many gynecologic procedures require a general anesthesia for example salpingec-
    tomy hysterectomy and laparotomy

Unit 9: Compound Words and Hyphenation

Review Exercises

Short Answers

1. When are hyphens unnecessary when using compound words? Give two examples.

   _____

   _____

   _____

2. When should you use hyphens with prefixes? Give two examples.

   _____

   _____

   _____

3. When should you use a hyphen to connect a compound adjective? Give an example.

   _____

   _____

   _____

4. When should you not use a hyphen with a compound adjective? Give an example.

   _____

   _____

   _____

5. Name the four word parts that always need hyphenation when forming a compound word. Label each word part either suffix or prefix.

   _____

   _____

   _____

6. Explain the rules for hyphenating follow-up, work-up and check-up.

   _____

   _____

   _____

7. Give two examples of using hyphens with compound numbers.

    _____

    _____

    _____

8. Give two examples of using hyphens with coined compound words

    _____

    _____

    _____

9. Give two examples of using hyphens wtih prefixes and suffixes.

    _____

    _____

    _____

10. Give two examples of using hyphens with number ranges.

    _____

    _____

    _____

Revision Exercise

Rekey and revise any of the following sentences which are incorrect in terms of hyphenation. If a sentence is correct, type "correct" in parentheses following the number of that sentence, and do not retype the sentence.

1. The chairman-elect was at the hospital board meeting.

2. She was a well developed, well nourished, Hispanic female.

3. Dr. Jackson will follow-up with the patient next week.

4. The patient had extremely low self esteem.

5. On Friday he had a small-bowel removal.

6. There was a perforation at the junction of the anterior two thirds with the posterior one third of the canal.

7. The white count showed 4-5 white blood cells per high-power field.

8. Last evening the patient had a nose-bleed, and last week she had an ear-ache.

9. The incision was recreated.

10.   Hearing loss is often high-frequency.

11.   The right sided acoustic neuroma was poorly-differentiated.

12.   Salpingo-oophorectomy can be a complicated and slow-healing operative procedure.

13.   His outdated medical practices were certainly nonEuropean.

14.   She was up-to-date on her immunizations, yet she was chronically-ill.

15.   She is to have the 3-0 Vicryl sutures removed next week at her check-up.

Unit 10: Contractions and Shortened Word Forms

Review Exercises

Short Answers

1. Name four contractions that take an apostrophe.

   _____

   _____

   _____

2. Name three contractions that do not take an apostrophe.

   _____

   _____

   _____

3. Which contractions are easily confused with similar personal pronouns?

   _____

   _____

   _____

4. When should you use contractions in medical transcription?

   _____

   _____

   _____

5. List five brief forms of words that are usually acceptable.

   _____

   _____

   _____

Revision Exercise

Rekey the following letter, changing contractions and brief forms of words when necessary.

Dear Dr. Martin:

Thank you for referring Judith, Mrs. Price's daughter. We
weren't able to see her yesterday as scheduled, cause we had
a couple of surgeries that took precedence. We did, however,
see her today, and she's a couple of problems of interest.

Her first problem's a positive Pap smear. It shows
questionable atypia, and we will do a lap sometime next week
if the second test comes back positive. We also need to
check her lytes and her sed rate. On palp during today's
exam, there was no discomfort or tenderness. Incidentally,
her vitals were normal.

Her second problem's an abnormal dermatitis. There's a 4 x 5
cm subcu lesion on the upper forearm that hasn't responded
to various meds. For this, I'll prescribe erythromycin tabs
or tetracycline caps for what I presume is a slight
infection, and then she'll apply hydrocortisone topically
for three days.

She'll fill her script as soon as possible, and I'll keep in
touch with you from time to time till then.

Sincerely,

Jack Booker, M.D.

Unit 11: Abbreviations

Review Exercises

Short Answers

1. Name three of the general rules for using abbreviations.

   _____

   _____

   _____

2. Name three of the general rules for not using abbreviations.

   _____

   _____

   _____

3. Explain how to make a capitalized abbreviation plural.

   _____

   _____

   _____

4. List eight uppercase abbreviations that should be spelled out when possible.

   _____

   _____

   _____

5. Explain how to make lowercase abbreviations plural.

   _____

   _____

   _____

6. Explain how to punctuate Latin abbreviations, and give three examples.

   _____

   _____

   _____

7. Explain the difference between abbreviating metric and English measurements.

   _____

   _____

   _____

8. Explain the rule for abbreviating with temperatures.

   _____

   _____

   _____

9. Explain the general guidelines for abbreviating with dates.

   _____

   _____

   _____

10. Name two of the rules for abbreviating with titles and degrees.

   _____

   _____

   _____

Special Exercise

Spell out the words for the following abbreviations:

1. ml _____

2. Dx _____

3. COPD _____

4. a.u. _____

5. q.i.d. _____

6. EOMI _____

7. ng _____

8. DTR _____

9. p.r.n. _____

10. WNL _____

11. CNS _____

12. t.i.d. _____

13. I&D _____

14. tsp. _____

15. I&O _____

16. O&P _____

17. p.c. _____

18. URI _____

19. 2PD _____

20. TIA _____

Unit 12: Capitalization

Review Exercises

Short Answers

1. List the rules for capitalizing medical report subject headings/subheadings.

    _____

    _____

    _____

2. What should you do if a sentence begins with a word that is not normally capitalized?

    _____

    _____

    _____

3. List the rules for capitalizing races, nationalities and languages.

    _____

    _____

    _____

4. List the rules for capitalizing after a colon.

    _____

    _____

    _____

5. What is an eponym, and when do you capitalize disease names?

    _____

    _____

    _____

6. . Provide three examples of capitalization of genus and species names.

    _____

    _____

    _____

7. Explain the rule for capitalizing Roman numerals.

_____

_____

_____

8. Explain the rule for capitalizing the names of drugs.

_____

_____

_____

9. Explain the rule for capitalizing abbreviations.

_____

_____

_____

10. Name four instances in which you should not use capitalization.

_____

_____

_____

Revision Exercise

Rekey the following report, using correct grammar, punctuation and capitalization. Consult previous units when necessary. Separate the two pages of the report in an appropriate manner.

History of Present Illness: patient is a White, married,
34-year-old female, who presented to the Emergency Room on
11/6/80 at 4:45 A.M. with a Chief Complaint of having chest
pain. The patient had called me about one half hour prior to
coming to the Emergency Room, stating she had chest pain
which was quite severe. Pain was located in the right
substernal area and seemed to radiate up towards the
sternocleidomastoid area of her neck at times. She had also
had an episode last thursday, november 3, when she was in
roanoke, virginia. She had another attack on Friday the 4th,
and then another episode on saturday the 5th, that was quite
severe.

PAST HISTORY: See the patient's past records for a complete
past medical history. She has a history of having childhood
Diabetes mellitus which is currently under control with
Insulin. Obstetrically, she is Gravida ii para ii ab 0. She
has had several recent bouts of hemophilus influenza, which
was responded to Penicillin. Her Mother died of a Myocardial
Infarction at age 55.

Continued

NANCY QUEST, M.D.   DAVIS, CHARLIE #290981
d&t:

History and Physical

Page 2

Laboratory data: C.B.C. showed unremarkable red cells, white
cells and platelets. Lytes showed a cholesterol of 182,
glucose of 92 and CO2 of 104. Urinalysis showed a specific
gravity of 1.009, a Ph of 5.9 and 2+ protein. EKG showed
some nonspecific ST-T wave changes. H&H were 14.2 and 43%
respectively.

Physical examination:
vitals: Temp was 99 Fahrenheit, respirations were 24, pulse
was 90 and BP was 120/94.
General: She is a well developed, well nourished, caucasian
female in moderate distress.
SKIN: Negative.
Head: patient is normocephalic and atraumatic.
Eyes: pupils equal, round and reactive to light and
accommodation. No nystagmus. No retinal hemorrhages.
EARS: the tympanic membranes are normal.
Nose: No signs of ecchymosis. Septum is normal.
Throat: No exudates or erythema. No evidence of Tonsillitis.
Cardiovascular: There is Tachycardia and Arrhythmia on
auscultation. There is a grade 2/6 Systolic murmur heard in
the fifth costal interspace. S3 sound is heard.
Abdomen: Soft, with active bowel sounds. No
Hepatosplenomegaly or Organomegaly. No rebound tenderness.
Extremities: No cyanosis, clubbing or edema.
Neurologic: Cranial nerves ii - xii are intact. DTR's are 2+
and equal. Motor and sensory exams is negative.

Impression:
1. Diabetes mellitus.
2. Unstable Angina.
3. Atrial Fibrillation.
4. Hypertensive cardiovascular disease.
5. Chronic hemophilus influenzae.

NANCY QUEST, M.D.   DAVIS, CHARLIE #290981
d&t:

History and Physical

Unit 13: Plural and Possessive Forms

Review Exercises

Short Answers

1. List the three rules for making non Latin or Greek words plural.

_____

_____

_____

2. Name the rule for making Greek or Latin-based words ending in "x" plural.

_____

_____

_____

3. Name the rule for making words ending in "a" plural.

_____

_____

_____

4. Name the rule for making words ending in "um" and words ending in "us" plural.

_____

_____

_____

5. Name the rule for making single letters and numbers plural.

_____

_____

_____

6. Name the two rules for making compound words plural.

_____

_____

_____

7. In what two ways can possession can be expressed?

    _____

    _____

    _____

8. Explain how to make singular nouns or names that end in "s" possessive.

    _____

    _____

    _____

9. Explain how to make plural nouns or names that end in "s" possessive.

    _____

    _____

    _____

10. List the two rules for making two or more words in a group show possession.

    _____

    _____

    _____

Revision Exercises

Revision Exercise #1

Rekey the following sentences, making the underlined words plural if they are singular or singular if they are plural, rewriting the sentences when necessary (use a medical dictionary if needed).

Example:

    The patient had a good prognosis. → The patients had good prognoses.

1. An arterial blood gas was drawn on the patient.
2. The appendix was sent to pathology for analysis.
3. The conjunctivae were pink.
4. An incision was made into the atrium.
5. A pebble was removed from the meati of the external auditory canal.
6. Computerized tomography showed an abnormality in the cerebellar culmina.

7. Microscopic <u>study</u> showed a <u>spermatozoon</u>.

8. Uterine <u>myomata</u> can be dangerous during pregnancy.

9. A <u>ventricornu</u> is an anatomical feature of the brain.

10. The interrogatories of the physician contained mostly <u>yes</u> and <u>no</u>.

11. Mrs. Mulberry is to take two tablets in the <u>a.m.</u>

12. The <u>nurse anesthetist</u> was present for the surgery.

13. The nose had no step-off and no <u>deformity.</u>

14. The <u>sergeant-at-arms</u> was on duty on the ship's infirmary.

15. The baby weighed <u>6 lb., 6 oz.</u>

Revision Exercise #2

Rekey the following sentences, making the underlined words possessive, rewriting the sentences when necessary.

Example:

She is the <u>friend of my mother</u>. She is my mother's friend.

1. The <u>symptoms of Judy, Marybeth and Peter</u> were identical.

2. The episodes were <u>of a duration of two days</u>.

3. Some <u>policies of insurance companies</u> request that the patient pay a copayment.

4. The <u>stethoscope belonging to Phyllis</u> was missing.

5. The <u>lounge for nurses</u> is at the end of the corridor.

6. The <u>meeting of the chairmen-of-the-board</u> was last night.

7. The desolate patient felt he was <u>the friend of no one</u>.

8. History taking is <u>the job of the nurse and the transcriptionist</u>.

9. Susan, <u>the niece of the Williamses</u>, recently graduated from medical school.

10. The elderly patient had only <u>pain medication for one day</u>.

11. <u>One complaint of his sister-in-law</u> was dysuria.

12. <u>The roommates of his brother</u> knew about the altercation.

13. The <u>margins of the calices</u> were not well defined.

14. The blood of Yusef and the bone marrow of Jasper were good matches.

15. Once again, the adolescent was late for the appointment with her doctor.

Unit 14: Numbers and Number Combinations

Review Exercises

Short Answers

1. Name three instances in which you should spell out a number.

   _____

   _____

   _____

2. Name three instances in which you should use figures.

   _____

   _____

   _____

3. Name two rules for using numbers with fractions.

   _____

   _____

   _____

4. Name three instances in which you should use Roman numerals.

   _____

   _____

   _____

5. Explain the rule for ordinal numerals.

   _____

   _____

   _____

6. Explain the rule for numbers with dates.

   _____

   _____

   _____

7. Explain the rule for numbers with ages.

_____

_____

_____

8. What symbols do you use in conjunction with numerals when describing sutures?

_____

_____

_____

9. Explain the rule with numbers and figures with drug values.

_____

_____

_____

10. Explain how a ratio is expressed in terms of numerals and signs.

_____

_____

_____

Fill in the Blanks

Use the correct number form of the numeral in parentheses (either arabic numeral, roman numeral or written number) to fill in the blank for each question, retyping the new sentence if necessary.

1. _____ milliliters of fluid was suctioned from the wound. (9)

2. The_____ -year-old was in for her well-baby check. (2)

3. The platelet count was _____. (330,000)

4. There were approximately _____ colonies of bacteria.
   (10,000,000)

5. _____ of all patients have a relapse. (1/3)

6. _____ out of _____ marriages do not end in divorce.
   (55, 100)

7. The infant was _____ weeks old. (5)

8. The differential showed _____ lymphs, _____
    bands and _____ segs. (8, 10, 65)

9. The dimensions of the sarcoma were _____.(3 millimeters by
    3½ millimeters)

10. There were _____ ketones in the urine. (0)

11. _____ degrees Celsius is the same as _____degrees
    Fahrenheit. (0, 32)

12. Blood lactate is normal when its value is between _____ and
    _____ . (.6, 1.8)

13. The hematocrit was _____. (43 percent)

14. Deep tendon reflexes were _____. (2 to 3 plus)

15. She was given a prescription for _____ mg of Tylenol _____,
    _____ to be taken for _____ days. (300, number
    3, 4 times a day, 7)

16. The FEV to FVC ratio was_____. (1 to 20)

17. His wound was closed with running _____ Mersilene and nylon
    sutures. (2 0, number 1)

18. Cranial nerve _____ was not functioning correctly. (5)

19. On cardiovascular examination there was a grade _____ sys-
    tolic ejection murmur appreciated. (3 out of 6)

20. The lipoma was stage _____. (2)

21. The surgery was done at _____; an incision was made in the
    _____ position. (8 o'clock in the morning, 9 o'clock)

22. The newborn's Apgar scores were _____ and _____
    at _____ and _____ minutes. (8, 10, 1, 5)

23. She had fractures of the _____, _____ and
    _____ lumbar vertebrae. (4th, 5th, 6th)

24. The cancer recurred on or around October _____ , _____, and went
    into remission the following June. (16th, 1980)

25. Tachyarrhythmia was noted on EKG from chest lead _____ and
    limb lead _____. (2, 4)

Unit 15: Commonly Confused Words, Misspelled Words and Spelling Hints

Review Exercises

Short Answers

1. Explain how commonly confused and misspelled words play a part in an employer's quality standards.

   _____

   _____

   _____

2. If your word processing program has spell checking, why do you need to know the difference between commonly confused words or misspelled words?

   _____

   _____

   _____

3. Name four frequently confused words that are not homonyms (words that are confused, but which do not sound alike).

   _____

   _____

   _____

4. Write down at least five commonly confused words you have used incorrectly from time to time, which you are unfamiliar with, or which might present special problems for you in the future. Learn the correct spelling and use of each word.

   _____

   _____

   _____

5. Write down at least five commonly misspelled words you have used incorrectly from time to time, which you are unfamiliar with, or which might present special problems for you in the future. Learn the correct spelling of each word.

   _____

   _____

   _____

6. Explain why you should not rely exclusively on pronunciation when spelling a word.

_____

_____

_____

7. Explain the complete "'i' before 'e'" rule.

_____

_____

_____

8. If you do not know whether a word uses an "ei" or an "ie" combination, and the "'i' before 'e'" rule does not apply, what should you do?

_____

_____

_____

9. Name the two exceptions to doubling the final consonant when adding a word ending.

_____

_____

_____

10. Of "manageable" and "managable," which is the correct word spelling and why?

_____

_____

_____

Identification

Circle all misspelled words. If the word is misspelled, write the correct spelling beside the incorrectly spelled word.

quandry	occuring	equipped	aquainted
auscultation	dependant	auxiliary	exagerate
liklihood	sacrilegious	diarhhea	forsee
assymetrical	judgement	ecchymosis	lisense
desiccated	annulus	bruwee	supersede

flegm	hemoptysis	sequellae	fascies
rhythm	Zanax	paroxysmal	vomitted
denies	ruff	theater	siezure
protien	fluorescein	concieve	frieght
piercing	tangible	beleive	equipped
throgh	tuff	canceled	codeine

Revision Exercise

In the following sentences, identify the underlined word and determine if it is a word that is incorrect and/or confused with another word. Identify wrong words by incorrect or illogical meanings. Rekey the sentences that contain a confused word, correcting the word in the revision. If the sentence is correct, type "CORRECT" beside the number of the correct sentence instead of retyping the sentence.

1. A metal rod was placed in the <u>ileum</u> to strengthen the bone.

2. The operative <u>sight</u> appeared to be well healed.

3. Her nutritional <u>regimen</u> included bran products twice a day.

4. The schizophrenic patient thought she was a queen; however, this was simply an <u>allusion.</u>

5. His <u>effect</u> was labile.

6. Although it seemed late, not much time had <u>past.</u>

7. Patients who have just had surgery are to remain <u>stationery</u> for a few days.

8. Consent forms should be signed <u>proceeding</u> the operation.

9. The new mother was given <u>anti-partum</u> pain medication.

10. His brother's <u>conscious</u> told him he should not have committed the act.

11. Gastrointestinal <u>reflux</u> can be an awful sensation.

12. There was a <u>discreet</u> mass located just beneath the pinna.

13. The otolaryngologist did an <u>oral</u> examination to check for hearing loss.

14. On admission to the coronary care unit, the patient was having heart <u>palpations.</u>

15. There was yellow-tinged <u>mucous</u> in the os.

16. Her main complaint was <u>petal</u> edema.

17. <u>Serous</u> fluid was emanating from the wound.

18. The limb was well <u>profused</u>.

19. Before the three-way x-ray, a <u>plane</u> film of the abdomen was taken.

20. The physician explained the <u>rational</u> for the surgery.

Unit 16: Editing Rules for the Medical Transcriptionist

Review Exercises

Short Answers

1. Name two instances in which you should edit.

   _____

   _____

   _____

2. Name two instances in which you should not edit.

   _____

   _____

   _____

3. Explain what needs to be taken into account when deciding whether or not to edit.

   _____

   _____

   _____

4. Explain how to support any editing changes you make.

   _____

   _____

   _____

5. If a physician spells out a word, why do you need to double check the spelling?

   _____

   _____

   _____

6. Explain what you should do if a physician constantly dictates in sentence fragments.

   _____

   _____

   _____

7. Explain what you should do if you cannot hear or understand a portion of dictation.

_____

_____

_____

8. Explain what you should do when a dictator does not share your writing style.

_____

_____

_____

9. How should you indicate that there is an error or inconsistency in a report?

_____

_____

_____

10. Explain the circumstances under which you should include two copies of a transcribed report back to the dictator for examination.

_____

_____

_____

Revision Exercise

Rekey the following report, editing when necessary and when acceptable.

OFFICE NOTE

SUBJECTIVE: This is a thirty-nine-year-old patient who we
saw today after a 3-year absence. We are seeing her back
because of a complaint of epistaxis. Prior to her current
complaints, he had moderate, red rhinitis for about month,
that has been treated by her primary care physician, Dr.
Elizabeth Marlow with antibiotics. Unfortunately, it
appears as though the antibiotic she has been taking she is
allergic to. After having had arrived home from work last
night, the patient started having intermittent epistaxis.
The patient called Dr. Marlow as soon as she came home. She
referred her to our office this morning.

OBJECTIVE: On examination, the patient has old dried blood
in both nares. There is no hemorrhages, exudates or erythema
noted at this time. She had mild nasal obstruction laying on
the examining table. The rest of her general head and neck
exam were clear.

ASSESSMENT: 1. Status post epistaxis, resolved
                2. Nasal obstruction, felt to be due to a URI.

PLAN: She will undergo cauterization as an outpatient in the
hospital on the morning. She will be placed on a new
antibiotic for her upper respiratory infection. She will
follow-up with Dr. Tucker or I within the next 4 days, and
she will see Dr. Marlow in her office after tomorrows
procedure.

Practice Tests

The six practice tests that follow are intended to prepare you for in-class examinations. Each practice test is based on cumulative knowledge acquired from a group of units. Each test question has only one correct answer. Select the correct answer, and write the correct corresponding alphabetical letter in the space provided. At the discretion of your instructor, the practice tests may be taken either after you have read the units covered in the test or after you have completed all exercises for units included in the test. The practice tests are designed for out-of-class use, but they may also be taken during class time. Consult with your instructor about how and when to take and submit the practice tests.

PRACTICE TEST #1 (Units 1-3)

_____ 1. The Greek physician Hippocrates:

A. used petroglyphs to document medical techniques

B. did not think confidentiality in the practice of medicine was important

C. wrote an oath that physicians take upon their entrance into the medical field

D. practiced medicine in the Stone Age

_____ 2. Medical transcriptionists:

A. never need to work independently or without supervision

B. are men and women who produce permanent and uniform medical information

C. are machines into which you put a audiocassette tape for transcribing

D. need not worry about the condition or appearance of their work stations

_____ 3. Which of the following is **not** a part of the audiocassette transcriber?

A. footpedal

B. base

C. headphones

D. monitor

_____ 4. A medical transcriptionist has the most contact with the physician in which of the following transcription environments?

A. a hospital

B. a medical office

C. a medical transcription service

D. none of the above

_____ 5. Which statement is correct?

A. 1 character equals about 1.5 bytes

B. 1 byte equals about 0.67 bits

C. 1 megabyte equals about 1024 bytes

D. 1 kilobyte equals about 1024 bits

_____ **6.** Which statement is correct?

    A. Microcomputer hardware comprises a printer, a CPU, a monitor and word processing programs.

    B. Microcomputer software comprises diskettes, a keyboard, reference books and materials such as templates.

    C. Floppy disks come in two sizes: 5¼-inch mini-diskettes and 3½-inch micro-diskettes.

    D. Hard disks are part of microcomputer software.

_____ **7.** Which statement is **not** correct?

    A. Writing to a diskette adds new information to it.

    B. Reading from a diskettes is when the drive examines data on the diskette and tells you something about that data.

    C. You may remove the diskette from the disk drive slot when the red light is on or the drive heads are spinning.

    D. You should not leave a diskette in the disk drive when turning the computer off.

_____ **8.** Formatting a diskette is doing which of the following:

    A. breaking down data on the diskette into partitions

    B. saving data to the diskette

    C. using a word processing system to save and retrieve data

    D. preparing a diskette to receive data

_____ **9.** Which of the following references would contain primarily listings of words without their definitions?

    A. a surgical word book

    B. a medical dictionary

    C. a _Physician's Desk Reference_

    D. a grammar guide

_____ **10.** Which of the following references would contain a complete definition for the word "rhinitis"?

    A. a pathology word book

    B. a medical dictionary

    C. a drug index

    D. a style guide

PRACTICE TEST #2 (Units 4-5)

_____ 1. Which of the following is **not** a title of one of the basic six types of reports?

A. the History of Present Illness Report

B. the Operative Note

C. the Pathology Report

D. the Discharge Summary

_____ 2. The focus of the Discharge Summary is which of the following?

A. the findings and description of procedures done in the hospital

B. the hospital course and final diagnoses

C. the history of present illness and laboratory data

D. the review of systems and physical examination

_____ 3. A sponge count and estimated blood loss would be included in which report?

A. the radiology report

B. the pathology report

C. the operative note

D. the consultation report

_____ 4. Which of the following hospital reports is usually dictated by the attending physician?

A. the consultation report

B. the discharge summary

C. the operative note

D. the pathology report

_____ 5. Which of the following would have a turnaround time of 12 hours or less?

A. a history and physical report

B. a discharge summary

C. a consultation report

D. a radiology report

_____   **6.** Which of the following statements is true regarding medical office patients?

     A. In medical offices, a patient's initial visit is usually a work-up.

     B. In medical offices, patients are usually seen at less frequent intervals than in hospitals.

     C. In medical offices, patients receive short-term treatment and usually do not return for another visit.

     D. In medical offices, a patient's initial visit is usually a follow-up.

_____   **7.** Which of the following statements is **not** correct?

     A. The check-up visit is made on three levels: the symptoms, the signs and the diagnosis.

     B. On the work-up visit the physician will usually narrate the patient's history, a physical examination, an assessment and a plan.

     C. The follow-up visit is the visit when a physician re-evaluates and re-examines the patient.

     D. A check-up is usually performed on a patient whose history is already known.

_____   **8.** In the "HPIP" chart note format, the impression is equivalent to what in the "SOAP" format?

     A. the objective

     B. the subjective

     C. the assessment

     D. the plan

_____   **9.** Fully justified text in correspondence is:

     A. where text lines up on the right margin

     B. where text lines up on the left margin

     C. where text is evenly spaced, but is ragged on the left and right margins

     D. where text is evenly spaced between and lines up on the left and right margins

_____   **10.** Which of the following statements about correspondence is correct?

     A. In open punctuation the complimentary close is punctuated with a comma.

     B. If a letter is too short to divide the last paragraph correctly, you can condense the letter on the first page by removing spaces.

     C. "Widows" are a type of salutation.

     D. The complimentary close and the signature block may stand alone on a page only if you use a photocopy notation.

PRACTICE TEST #3 (Units 6-8)

_____ 1. Which of the following is <u>not</u> correct?

   A. Phonetics are sound breakdowns of a word.

   B. Acronyms are the opposites of words.

   C. Etymology is the breakdown of a word into Latin and Greek roots, suffixes and prefixes.

   D. Homonyms are words that are sound alike.

_____ 2. Using etymology clues, which of the following is the correct definition of "cholelithotomy"?

   A. surgical incision to remove a gallstone

   B. inflammation of the gallbladder

   C. surgical removal of the uterus

   D. infection of the eyes

_____ 3. Which of the following word groups are homonyms?

   A. laser/scuba

   B. discreet/discrete

   C. anterior/posterior

   D. cardiovascular/heart and vessels

_____ 4. Which of the following word groups are synonyms?

   A. two/too

   B. dopa/AIDS

   C. hypertensive/hypotensive

   D. disease/pathology

_____ 5. Which of the following sentences is grammatically correct?

   A. The nurse lied a blanket on the patient.

   B. Everyday Mrs. Taylor sets out in the sun.

   C. If I were rich, I would add a new wing to the hospital.

   D. Shut up!

6. Which of the following statements is **not** correct?

   A. Nouns are used more frequently than any other part of speech.

   B. Objects receive the action of a verb.

   C. Personal pronouns are noun substitutes that refer to a particular person or a group of people.

   D. "That" always introduces nonrestrictive clauses, or clauses that are nonessential to preserve the meaning of a sentence.

7. Which of the following sentences uses indefinite pronouns correctly?

   A. Somebody had their records confused with yours.

   B. Each surgeon uses their own special techniques.

   C. Either the counselor or the psychiatrist counsel patients on Wednesday.

   D. Neither the physician nor the surgeon considers surgery the best alternative.

8. Which of the following sentences uses punctuation correctly?

   A. The left-sided bright yellow rhinitis was not purulent; however, it was noticeable.

   B. The child was sick, his mother took him to the hospital.

   C. "Disrobe and put on the gown"! the nurse commanded.

   D. The student asked "Can transcriptionists earn a good salary?"

9. Which of the following sentences does **not** use punctuation correctly?

   A. Type the following on the report: the patient's name, and that of his mother, father and siblings; the patient's medical record number; and the date of the patient's discharge.

   B. Her patient was in labor; however, the nurse went home.

   C. There was no doubt about it, the disease was terminal.

   D. The nurse thought she saw an "apparition"!

10. Which of the following sentences uses correct grammar and punctuation?

    A. Neither Thomas nor I approve of the patient's treatment.

    B. The incision, that was thought not to be deep enough by the physician, was irrigated.

    C. The extremities were negative, however, the neurological exam is positive for some hypesthesia.

    D. Sit the patient's file on the counter immediately!

PRACTICE TEST #4 (Units 9-11)

_____ 1. Which of the following sentences follows the rules for compound nouns?
   A. The reexamination showed metastasis.
   B. The operative technique was nonAmerican.
   C. A nose bleed is the layman's term for an epistaxis.
   D. She was given a regimen of anti-inflammatories.

_____ 2. Which of the following sentences follows the rules for compound adjective?
   A. The specimen was coagulase positive.
   B. His toddler, although undernourished, is well-developed.
   C. The freely-flowing drain was tightly clamped.
   D. Presbycusis often is manifested by a high frequency hearing loss.

_____ 3. Which of the following sentences uses use hyphenation correctly?
   A. Dr. Porter should see the patient in two-three days.
   B. It was obvious that the patient had consumed more than one fifth of a bottle of whiskey.
   C. We will adopt a watch and wait attitude.
   D. Suture removal will be in 10-12 days.

_____ 4. Which of the following sentences does **not** use the follow-up/work-up/check-up rule correctly?
   A. Mr. Thompson's check-up is scheduled for next month.
   B. Though the disease was thoroughly worked up, no diagnosis could be given.
   C. Please follow-up with Dr. Orion tomorrow morning.
   D. The workup was incomplete.

_____ 5. Which of the following is a correct contraction?
   A. a'int
   B. they're
   C. whose
   D. alot

_____ 6. Which of the following contractions should take an apostrophe?
   A. maam
   B. almost
   C. their
   D. till

_____ **7.** Which of the following brief forms is acceptable to use?

    A. subcu

    B. vitals

    C. lytes

    D. preop

_____ **8.** It is acceptable to use abbreviations:

    A. in diagnoses

    B. with most laboratory data

    C. when a quantity of measurement is unknown

    D. if the abbreviation is not dictated

_____ **9.** Select the correct abbreviation and what word(s) it represents:

    A. A&P - as soon as possible

    B. H&H - hemoglobin and hematocrit

    C. T&A - therapy and adenoidectomy

    D. O&P - oscillation and percussion

_____ **10.** Which of the following statements is correct?

    A. You must always include both the words "degree" and either "Fahrenheit" or "Celsius" when transcribing a temperature; it is never appropriate to use only the numeral to indicate degrees.

    B. Metric abbreviations use lowercase or capital and lowercase with periods.

    C. To make a lowercase abbreviation plural, delete the periods and add an apostrophe + "s".

    D. It is acceptable to use both a social title before a name and a professional title afterwards concurrently in medical transcription.

PRACTICE TEST #5 (Units 12-14)

_____ 1. Which of the following sentences correctly uses capitalization?

A. Extremities: there is no clubbing, cyanosis or edema.

B. Ph of the urine was 6.5.

C. The patient was an Hispanic female psychologist.

D. The sequelae of the disease included the following: Infection, gangrene, necrosis and amputation.

_____ 2. Which of the following sentences does **not** correctly use capitalization?

A. The discharge diagnoses included Staph aureus, Escherichia coli, chronic obstructive pulmonary disease, congestive heart failure and Diabetes mellitus.

B. Motrin is a brand name for the drug ibuprofen.

C. The patient's mother was present for the exam.

D. She was gravida III, para II, AB I.

_____ 3. Which of the following statements is **not** correct?

A. Place a capitalized article before the word "patient" when it is dictated alone at the beginning of a sentence.

B. When listing system components in the physical examination, capitalize the first letter of every word following the colon.

C. Capitalize the first letter of eponyms.

D. When abbreviations are capitalized, you should not usually use periods.

_____ 4. Which of the following words is in the correct plural form?

A. reticulums

B. appendectomies

C. symptoma

D. diagnosises

_____ 5. Which of the following words is in the correct plural form?

A. calyxes

B. fibromas

C. data

D. algaes

_____ 6. Which of the following sentences contains an incorrect plural form?

    A. Diethylstilbestrol was given to many pregnant women in the 1950's and 1960's.

    B. The medical chiefs of staff were present for the meeting.

    C. The child weighed 36 lb.

    D. Two of the attorney-at-laws were also physicians.

_____ 7. Which of the following sentences correctly uses the possessive form?

    A. The ladies' room is on the second floor.

    B. The new physician had not yet encountered many childrens' illnesses.

    C. Sally, John and Bill's parents were all present for the explanation of the surgical risks.

    D. Her pain lasted for six minute's time.

_____ 8. Which of the following sentences does **not** correctly use the possessive form?

    A. Bert Parks's rendition of "Here she is, Miss America" resulted in lacrimation from several audience members.

    B. The Women's Center was opened last week.

    C. The boys' mothers spent the night at the hospital.

    D. Large medical corporation's have an obligation to their patients.

_____ 9. Which of the following sentences uses numbers correctly?

    A. 2,500 people were present at the symposium.

    B. His two-year-old sister had varicella.

    C. The laceration measured 5 cm in length.

    D. Seven out of 10 of the children had developed the symptoms.

_____ 10. Which of the following sentences does **not** use numbers correctly?

    A. Ten percent of the two billion people in the United States have this disease.

    B. Studies have shown that 2/3 of patients treated are responsive to the therapy.

    C. The blood consisted of 3% eosinophils.

    D. Two 3-0 Vicryl sutures were used to close the wound.

PRACTICE TEST #6 (Units 15-16)

_____ 1. Which of the following statements is correct?

    A. Medical transcriptionists rarely have a problem with confused or misspelled words.

    B. Misspelled words will be flagged when a document is spell checked on a word processor.

    C. Confused words will be flagged when a document is spell checked on a word processor.

    D. Confused or misspelled words have no effect on an employers or a client's quality standards.

_____ 2. Which of the following sentences contains a confused word?

    A. The patient had no pedal edema.

    B. She was given two pints of packed red blood cells.

    C. The stimulus may not illicit a response.

    D. Posterior and anterior views of the chest were shown on x-ray.

_____ 3. Which of the following sentences does **not** contain a confused word?

    A. A spinal innovation problem was thought to be responsible for the hemiplegia.

    B. Two internasal polyps were removed.

    C. Her mental status examination revealed that she had a depressed affect.

    D. Examination of the patient's neck showed no knuckle rigidity.

_____ 4. Choose the only correct word for the blank: **The _____ patient, whose temperature was 98.6, was discharged.**

    A. rationale

    B. unanimous

    C. plane

    D. afebrile

_____ 5. Choose the only correct word for the blank: **The patient was _____.**

    A. stationery

    B. conscience

    C. prostrate

    D. rationale

_____ 6. Which of the following words is spelled correctly?

  A. guiac

  B. occurred

  C. auxilliary

  D. dessicated

_____ 7. Which of the following words is **not** spelled correctly?

  A. judgment

  B. miniature

  C. opthalmology

  D. accommodation

_____ 8. Which of the following words is **not** an exception to the "**I** before **e**, except after **c**. . ." rule?

  A. freight

  B. protein

  C. codeine

  D. seizure

_____ 9. Which of the following statements is **not** true?

  A. Do not edit to reflect your own personal writing style; you are not the author of the transcription.

  B. Always leave a blank when you cannot hear or understand some part of a dictation.

  C. Always be prepared to support your editing changes.

  D. You can always trust a dictator's spelling.

_____ 10. Which of the following sentences should **not** be edited or flagged?

  A. The patient, who was thoroughly worked up last week, was noted to have a polyp while lying on the table.

  B. Her blood count showed a white blood count of 320,000 and a platelet count of 11,500.

  C. The patient will follow-up with either Dr. Miller or I sometime next week.

  D. On examination, there is no abnormalities.

Appendices

Appendix A

DOS/WordPerfect Features

A-1 DOS (Disk Operating System), Directory and File Manipulation Features

Functions are specific tasks you can ask the computer to do. Functions are performed by giving the computer commands. Internal commands [I.C.] are resident commands, or commands that reside on the buffer of the computer system in the central processing unit (CPU). You may use internal commands every time your computer is booted up. External commands [E.C.] are transient commands, or commands that are stored on a DOS disk or another kind of operating systems disk, and you must have an operating system diskette in the disk drive (or DOS copied onto the hard drive) in order to use external commands. Commands can be keyed either in lowercase or uppercase.

(~ signifies depression of the space bar, ↵ signifies return or enter)

Basic Commands for Dual Floppy Disk Users

Check Status of a Disk's Contents	**CHKDSK~A:** ↵ (this command checks the status of files on the A disk)
	CHKDSK~B: ↵ (this command checks the status of files on the B disk) [E.C.]
Clear the Screen	**CLS** ↵ (commands computer to clear the screen at the disk drive prompt and display the disk drive prompt on an otherwise blank screen) [I.C.]
Copy	**COPY~A:*.*~B:** ↵ (commands computer to copy everything from the A disk to the B disk)
	COPY~A:*.MAC~B: ↵ (commands computer to copy everything on the A disk with an ending, or extension, of .MAC to the B disk)

To do this function:	Type this command at A> (A:\>) (the A disk drive prompt) or B> (B:\>) (the B disk drive prompt):
Copy (Cont'd)	**COPY~B:1MT1024A.*~A:** ↵ (commands computer to copy everything on the B disk beginning, or with a prefix, of 1MT1024A. to the A disk)
	COPY~A:\ASSIGN*.EXE~A:\FORMATS ↵ (commands computer to copy everything with the file extension .EXE in the ASSIGN subdirectory on the A disk to the FORMATS subdirectory on the A disk) {See A-4, File Names and Name Extensions, below} [I.C.]
Date	**DATE ~ 01-01-90** ↵ (commands computer to change the date in its memory to the date you type in after returning) [I.C.]
Delete	**DEL~A:*.*** ↵ (commands computer to erase everything on the A disk)
	DEL~A:*.EXE ↵ (commands computer to erase everything on the A disk with an .EXE extension) {See erase below} [I.C.]
Directory	**DIR** ↵ (commands computer to display the directory of the disk in the drive of the prompt that is displayed)
	DIR~A: ↵ (commands computer to display the directory of the A disk, whether you are at B or A)
	DIR~B: ↵ (commands computer to display the directory of the B disk, whether you are at B or A)
	DIR/W ↵ (commands computer to display the directory in a wide mode, stopping the display at the end of each screen, without the byte amounts listed)
	DIR/P ↵ (commands computer to display the directory in a page, or screen, mode, stopping the display at the end of each page) [I.C.]
Erase	**ERASE~A:*.*** ↵ (commands computer to erase everything on the A disk; press Y to confirm erasure)
	ERASE~A:*.EXE ↵ (commands computer to erase everything on the A disk with an .EXE suffix) [I.C.]
Format	**FORMAT~B:** ↵ (commands computer to format the B disk to receive data)

To do this function:	Type this command at A> (A:\>) (the A disk drive prompt) or B> (B:\>) (the B disk drive prompt):
Format (Cont'd)	**FORMAT~B:/S** ↵ (commands computer to format the B disk for the potential to have an operating system copied onto it) **FORMAT~B:/V** ↵ (commands computer to format as well as name the B disk) [E.C.]
Format and Copy Disk	**DISKCOPY~A:~B:** ↵ (commands computer to use the DOS diskette in the A drive to format the disk in the B drive, as well as copy everything from the A disk to the B disk
Pause Scrolling	**<Ctrl> + "S"** simultaneously (commands computer to stop or restart scrolling, e.g., after giving a **DIR** command, to control display of the directory and prevent it from scrolling down the screen too quickly to observe, use the pause scrolling command) [I.C.]
Rename	**REN~A:1MT1024A~B:1MT1024B**↵ (commands computer to rename the file named "1mt1024a" on the A disk to a new file named "1mt1024b" on the B disk) [I.C.]
Soft Boot	press the **<Ctrl> + <Alt> + <Delete>** keys simultaneously (commands computer to boot up without turning the computer off manually; this command is often used when the keyboard "locks" or "freezes", or a command executed within a software program is not working correctly and you must exit and re-enter the computer system) [I.C.]
Time	**time** ↵ **12:30** (commands computer to change the time in its memory to the time you type in after returning) [I.C.]

Basic Commands for Hard Disk Drive Users

(Note: Most hard disk drives use the C drive as the primary drive — the drive where DOS is located; your computer may use the C drive, or another drive such as the D drive, the E drive, the F drive or the G drive as the primary drive.)

To do this function:	Type this command at C> (C:\>) (the C disk drive prompt):
Check Status of a Disk's Contents	**CHKDSK~C:** ↵ (this command checks the status of files on the C disk)

To do this function:	Type this command at C> (C:\>) (the C disk drive prompt):
Check Disk Status (Cont'd)	**CHKDSK~A:** ↵ (this command checks the status of files on the A disk)
Clear the Screen	**CLS** ↵ (commands computer to clear the screen at the C drive prompt and display the C drive prompt on an otherwise blank screen)
Copy	**COPY~A:*.*~C:** ↵ (commands computer to copy everything from the A disk to the C drive)
	COPY~C:*.MAC~A: ↵ (commands computer to copy everything on the C disk with an ending, or extension, of .MAC to the A disk)
	COPY~A:1MT1024A.*~C: ↵ (commands computer to copy everything on the A disk beginning, or with a prefix, of 1MT1024A. to the C drive)
	COPY~C:\ASSIGN*.EXE~C:\FORMATS ↵ (commands computer to copy everything with the file extension .EXE in the ASSIGN subdirectory on the C drive to the FORMATS subdirectory on the C drive) {See A-4, File Names and Name Extensions, below} [I.C.]
Date	**DATE ~ 01-01-90** ↵ (commands computer to change the date in its memory to the date you type in after returning) [I.C.]
Delete	**DEL~A:*.*** ↵ (commands computer to erase everything on the A disk)
	DEL~C:*.EXE ↵ (commands computer to erase everything on the C disk with an .EXE extension) {See erase below}
Directory	**DIR** ↵ (commands computer to display the directory of the disk in the drive of the prompt that is displayed)
	DIR~A: ↵ (commands computer to display the directory of the A disk, whether you are at B or A)
	DIR~B: ↵ (commands computer to display the directory of the B disk, whether you are at B or A)
	DIR/W ↵ (commands computer to display the directory in a wide mode, stopping the display at the end of each screen, without the byte amounts listed)

To do this function:	**Type this command at C> (C:\>) (the C disk drive prompt):**
Directory (Cont'd)	**DIR/P** ↵ (commands computer to display the directory in a page, or screen, mode, stopping the display at the end of each page) [I.C.]
Erase	**ERASE~A:*.*** ↵ (commands computer to erase everything on the A disk; press Y to confirm erasure);
	ERASE~C:*.EXE ↵ (commands computer to erase everything on the A disk with an .EXE suffix) [I.C.]
Format	**FORMAT~A:** ↵ (commands computer to format the A disk to receive data)
	FORMAT~A:/S ↵ (commands computer to format the A disk for the potential to have an operating system copied onto it)
	FORMAT~A:/V ↵ (commands computer to format as well as name the A disk)
Format and Copy from Hard Disk	**DISKCOPY~A:** ↵ (commands computer to format the disk in the A drive as well as copy everything on the C drive to the A disk
Pause Scrolling	**\<Ctrl\> + "S"** simultaneously (commands computer to stop or restart scrolling, e.g., after giving a **DIR** command, to control display of the directory and prevent it from scrolling down the screen too quickly to observe, use the pause scrolling command) [I.C.]
Rename	**REN~C:1MT1024A~A:1MT1024B**↵ (commands computer to rename the file named "1mt1024a" on the A disk to a new file named "1mt1024b" on the B disk) [I.C.]
Soft Boot	press the **\<Ctrl\> + \<Alt\> + \<Delete\>** keys simultaneously (commands computer to boot up without turning the computer off manually; this command is often used when the keyboard: "locks" or "freezes", or a command executed within a software program is not working correctly and you must exit and re-enter the computer system) [I.C.]
Time	**time** ↵ **12:30** (commands computer to change the time in its memory to the time you type in after returning) [I.C.]

Commands For Dos Directory Manipulation

To do this function:	Type this command at C: (C:\>) (the C disk drive prompt), or A: (A:\>) or B: (B:\>) (the A or B disk drive prompt):
Make a Directory	MD\HOMEWORK ↵ (commands computer to make a new directory called "homework")
Change Directory	CD\HOMEWORK ↵ (commands computer to change the directory to the "homework" directory) CD\ ↵ (commands computer to change the directory to the root, or main, directory)
Remove Directory	RD\HOMEWORK (commands computer to remove the directory named "homework") [Note: you cannot remove a directory while in the directory you want to remove; you must first change the directory to the root directory. Also, you can only remove an empty directory, and you cannot remove the main directory.]

Symbols Used in Dos

Symbol	Name and Use
\	**Backslash.** This signifies the main directory, directory change or separates (sub)directory name from file name (e.g., A:\SUBDIR\FILENAME).
>	**Prompt.** This signifies the disk drive, whether A or B (floppy disk drives) or C (a hard disk drive).
*	**Wildcard/global character.** Signifies one or more characters. (See section A-4, below.)
–	**Cursor.** This flashing bar tells you where your next character will be typed.

A-2   WordPerfect Features

Commonly Used Function Keys	Description
F1	Cancel (brings back your last deletion, or the one previous to it)

Commonly Used Function Keys	Description
ALT-F1	Thesaurus (finds synonyms for a specified word)
F2	Forward search (searches for a character string forward from the cursor)
ALT-F2	Global search and replace (searches for a character string forward from the cursor, and replaces it with specified text)
SHIFT-F2	Backward search (searches for a character string backward from the cursor)
CTRL-F2	Spell (checks spelling and gives spelling hints)
F3	Help (helps you with function keys and other WP features)
ALT-F3	Reveal codes (reveals on the lower portion of the screen codes word perfect uses to aid you in locating such operations as centered text, bolded text, underlined text, hard and soft pages, hard returns, etc.)
SHIFT-F3	Switch (switches from document 1 to document 2, and vice versa)
CTRL-F3	Screen (lets you split a screen into two documents [as in switch]; lets you draw lines using the line draw feature)
F4	Indent (indents whole paragraph - to the next hard return - in the amount of spaces of one tab setting or more)
ALT-F4	Block (highlights a portion of text or a code for manipulation)
SHIFT-F4	Right and left indent (indents both from the right and left margins the amount of space of one or more tab settings)
CTRL-F4	Move (moves, copies or otherwise manipulates a blocked portion of text or code)
F5	List files (lists in directory form the contents of a disk)
SHIFT-F5	Date (inserts the date you entered in DOS into text)
CTRL-F5	Text In/Out (saves text in the DOS format [without codes], in another word processor's format, or in a lower WordPerfect version format)
F6	Bold (makes marked portion of text bold when printed)
ALT-F6	Flush right (makes text line up on the right margin instead of on the left; the left side is jagged)
SHIFT-F6	Center (centers marked portion of text)

**Commonly Used
Function Keys**   **Description**

F7	Exit (exits Word Perfect after asking if you want the document to be saved or not)
SHIFT-F7	Print (sends document on the screen to the printer)
F8	Underline (underlines marked portion of text when printed)
ALT-F8	Page format [WP 4.2] (makes formatting changes such as page numbering, headers and footers, top margin, etc.); Style [WP 5.0-5.1] (changes the formats in a manner called a style, to be retrieved whenever you want those particular format settings)
SHIFT-F8	Line format [WP 4.2] (makes formatting changes such as line spacing, hyphenation, margin settings, tab settings, etc.); Format [WP 5.0-5.1] (all formats, including formats for page, line, print, and other special settings, are made on this one key in WP 5.0 & 5.1)
CTRL-F8	Print format [WP 4.2] (makes printing formatting changes, such as justification, etc.); Font [WP 5.0] (makes changes in the print size, style, and appearance)
F9-KEYS	Merge (lets you combine items in two or more documents using codes) and Graphics (lets you import graphics from publishing software programs or create graphs, boxes, etc.)
F10	Save (saves document without exiting Word Perfect)
ALT-F10	Macro (executes a macro you have previously defined)
SHIFT-F10	Retrieve (retrieves a document on disk)
CTRL-F10	Macro define (defines or creates a macro using an abbreviation)

A-3   Cursor Control

To get to:	Press these keys (on numerical pad):
Beginning of the document	Home + Home + ↑
Beginning of the line	Home + Home + ←
One character to the left	←

To get to:	Press these keys (on numerical pad):
One character to the right	→
End of the document	Home + Home + ↓
End of the line	End —or— Home + Home + →
One line down	↓
One line up	↑
One full page down	PgDn
One full page up	PgUp

To do this:	Press these keys:
Move one screen down	+ on numerical pad —or— Home + ↓
Move one screen up	− on numeric pad —or— Home + ↑
Move one word to the left	Ctrl + ←
Move one word to the right	Ctrl + →
Delete to end of line	Ctrl + End
Delete to end of page	Ctrl + PgDn
Delete a word	Ctrl + Backspace
Make a hard page	Ctrl + Enter (Return)
Get into typeover mode	Ins
Delete characters before the cursor	Backspace
Delete characters on or after cursor	Del

WordPerfect Cursor/Movement Commands

To do this:	Press these keys:
Undo your last deletion	F1 and then either 1 for the most recent deletion or 2 for a previous deletion

Create a macro	Ctrl-F10 before and after defining the macro
Execute (do) a macro	Alt-F10 and type the abbreviation
Change the default directory	F5, =, then type the new directory name; type "Y" to create a new directory, and press enter —or— F5, press enter, type "7"; type the new directory name; type "Y" to create a new directory, and press enter
Change to another directory	F5, =; type the other directory name, and then press enter twice —or— F5, press enter, type "7"; cursor down to the other directory or type the name of the other directory, and press enter twice
Get back to the document screen from the directory screen	F1 (cancel) —or— F7 (exit) —or— type the number displayed at the bottom of the directory screen that tells you to exit
Exit a document and save it	F7
Save a document without exiting	F10

A-4   File Names and Name Extensions

Files consist of two parts: a primary file name and an extension. The primary file name is made up of one to eight characters. The primary file name is necessary to each file. The extension, which is not required, but which is helpful in organizing like files, is made up of one to three characters. The primary file name is separated from the extension by a period (.). If the primary file name consists of seven or fewer characters, DOS will place spaces in the remaining character slots before the period in the directory. If the file name does not contain an extension, you may call up the file name without utilizing the period. If the file name, however, does contain an extension, a period is necessary to separate the primary file name from the extension. When you name a file, you can use uppercase or lowercase characters, although when you see the file name in the directory or listed, you will usually see that file name in uppercase characters. You may call up the file name using either lowercase or uppercase characters. The characters used in the primary file name as well as the extension can be nearly any character you choose on the keyboard. There are, however, some exceptions. Following are the valid and invalid file name characters:

Valid file name characters:

The letters "A" through "Z" (upper or lower case)

The numerals "0" through "9"

These symbols: ! @ # $ % ^ & ( ) - _ { } ~ '

Invalid file name characters:

These symbols: * + = ? / . , < > ; : "

The asterisk symbol (*) is used to denote a wildcard character. It is also referred to as "global" or "everything", as * can signify one or more characters or all characters. However, the asterisk can only represent an entire primary file name, the entire extension of a file name, or the last characters in either a file name or extension. The question mark (?) is also a wildcard character. Unlike the asterisk, however, it can usually signify only one character at a time. (The expression ????????.??? is equivalent to the expression *.*). You must use the question mark if you are indicating a wildcard character that begins a primary file name where other characters follow in the primary file name. Following are examples of the use of the asterisk and the question mark. If you have a diskette (diskette A:) containing these files:

WP.EXE	WP.FIL	WP{WP}US.SUP	WP{WP}US.DIC
WP.DIC	TT.EXE	TT.FIL	
TT.HLP	TT.11	TT.22	

1. To copy (you may also use delete, erase, etc.) all files from diskette A: to diskette B:, type: **copy~a:*.*~b:** ↵

2. To copy all files ending in .EXE from A: to B:, type: **copy~a:*.exeb:**↵

3. To copy all files containing only WP in the primary filename from A: to B:, type: **copy~a:wp.*~b:** ↵

4. To copy all files containing WP as part of the primary filename from A: to B:, type: **copy~a:wp*.*~b:** ↵

5. To copy all files containing {WP} in the primary filename from A: to B:, type: **copy~a:??{wp}*.*~b:** ↵

6. To copy all files containing only two characters in the primary file name, type: **copy~a:??.*~b:** ↵

7. To copy all files containing only two characters in the primary file name and two characters in the extension, type: **copy~a:??.??b:** ↵

In addition, DOS commonly uses certain file name extensions for specific uses or purposes. Following are some common extensions and the type of the file (use or purpose) containing the extension.

Extension	File Type
BAK	backup file
BK!	backup file
BAT	batch file (a command file that performs certain tasks; usually in order to execute the command, you need only type the letters in the primary file name of the .BAT file, e.g., to execute the AUTOEXEC.BAT batch file command, you would simply type "autoexec" followed by return at the prompt)
BIN	binary file for use with DOS
COM	command file for use with DOS
DAT	ASCII data file (ASCII means common keyboard characters)
DOC	ASCII document file
EXE	executable file (usually in order to execute the command, you need only type the letters in the primary file name of the .EXE file, e.g., to get into Word Perfect, you execute the WP.EXE command by simply typing "wp" and return at the prompt)
LIB	library code file
LST	ASCII list file
OVR	overlay file
SYS	system file (these files are necessary to the proper operation of the disk drive system; do not remove files containing these extensions)
$$$	temporary work file

Appendix B

Glossary of Common Medical Terms

accommodation: adjustment of the eye to distance

akathisia: a condition of motor restlessness; inability to remain inactive

allergen: a substance that induces hypersensitivity

amenorrhea: absence or cessation of menses

analgesic: a substance that relieves pain

anemia: a condition of having below the normal amount of erythrocytes

anesthetic: a substance that causes a loss of feeling or sensation, or that produces unconsciousness

angina: a condition producing severe pain and constriction of the heart that is a result of an insufficient blood supply to the heart

antibiotic: destructive of a living substance; a chemical microorganism substance that has the ability to destroy other microorganisms

antibody: an immunoglobulin molecule that interacts with or reacts to an antigen

antidote: a substance that counteracts a poison or a drug

anxiety: a feeling of unwarranted apprehension, uncertainty and/or fear, associated with physiological changes

Apgar score: a method of rating a newborn's physical condition at one minute and five minutes after birth, including appearance (color), pulse (heart rate), grimacing (stimulation response), activity (muscle tone) and respiratory rate

aphasia: inability to speak

apnea: a period of cessation of breathing

appendiceal: pertaining to the appendix, or a dependent part of an attached structure

arrhythmia: irregular or loss of rhythm of the heart

arthritis: inflammation of the joints

asthma: a condition of recurrent attacks of paroxysmal dyspnea with wheezing and bronchial spasms

astringent: a substance that contracts, toughens, shrinks, whitens or hardens skin or tissue

asymmetry: a lack of symmetry; a lack of similar polar or axial proportionment

ataxia: a lack of muscular coordination

atelectasis: incomplete expansion or collapse of the lung

atraumatic: without evidence of trauma

atrophy: a degeneration or wasting away of something

auscultation: listening to sounds in the body, often times with a stethoscope

Babinski's reflex: flexion inward of the great toe when the sole of the foot is stimulated

bacteriuria: an excessive amount of bacteria in the urine

biliary: relating to bile

bilirubin: bile pigment

bradycardia: a slow heart beat rate

bronchitis: inflammation of the bronchi

bronchodilator: a medicinal device that dilates the bronchi of the lungs

bruit: an abnormal sound or noise

bursitis: inflammation of a bursa; inflammation of a saclike cavity filled with a viscous fluid where friction would otherwise develop

cafe au lait: (French - literally: coffee with milk) a spot on the skin that is the color of creamed coffee

carcinoma: a cancer; a malignant new growth composed of epithelial cells that tend to metastasize

cardiovascular: relating to the heart and vessels

caries: the molecular decay, decomposition or death of a bone, where it becomes soft, porous and discolored; a process which results in the destruction of a tooth, producing a cavity in the tooth

caruncle: a small fleshy eminence

catheterization: passage of a tube through the body for evacuating or injecting fluids into body cavities

caudal: pertaining to the tail or end of something

cauterization: cutting or destroying tissue with an electric, caustic, burning or freezing device

cerumen: ear wax

cholelithiasis: the presence or forming of gallstones

claudication: the quality of being limp

clonus: alternating rigidity and relaxation in rapid succession

coagulation:t   the process of clotting, especially blood

conjunctivitis: inflammation of the pink portion of the eyelids

coryza: a head cold

crepitation: the sound of rattling or crackling; the grating of bones together

cryocautery: surgical cutting using coldness

culmen: the top of the cerebellum

cutaneous: pertaining to the skin

cyanosis: a bluish or purplish discoloration of the skin, due to the deficiency of oxygen

cystitis: inflammation of the bladder

cystoscope: an instrument used for internal examination of the ureter and bladder

decubitus: the state of lying down; something pertaining to the state or act of lying down or being in bed

desiccate: to make thoroughly dry

diabetes mellitus: a disease in which the patient displays symptoms of excessive urination and signs of elevated sugar in the blood and urine that results from inadequate insulin processing

diagnosis: the determination of the functional state or a body organ or component; the act of distinguishing one disease from another

diaphoresis: an increase in perspiration

diarrhea: an abnormal frequency and fluid content of stools

diastolic pressure: the lower reading of the blood pressure; the period of least pressure in the arterial vascular system

diplopia: a condition of having double vision

diuretic: a substance that promotes or increases the secretion of urine

dorsal: pertaining to the back of something

dyspnea: difficulty breathing

dysuria: difficult or painful urination

ecchymosis: a bruise; a black-and-blue appearance caused by hemorrhaging under the skin

ectopic: out of place or malpositioned

eczema: an inflammatory disease of the skin accompanied by redness, itching and, if more severe, oozing and crusting

electrolytes: the ionized salts contained in the blood, serums and cells; in hematology, the salts including sodium, potassium, calcium, magnesium and chlorine

embolus: a blood clot lodged in a vessel, causing obstruction of blood flow

enuresis: involuntary urination; bed-wetting

epidermis: the outermost layer of skin

epistaxis: a nosebleed

equilibrium: a state of balance

erythema: a reddening, especially of the skin

erythrocyte: a red blood cell

etiology: the study of the factors that cause disease; the precipitants to a disease process

euphoria: a state or sense of well being; the absence of pain or distress

exophthalmos: an abnormal protrusion of the eyeball

exudate: material such as fluid, mucus, cells or cellular debris that has escaped from blood vessels and has been deposited in the tissue or tissue surfaces, usually as a result of inflammation

fibrillation: an abnormal electrical current or contraction, especially of the heart

fimbriated: being fringed or having fringed edges

fissure: a cleft, fold or groove, especially in the cerebral cortex

fistula: an abnormal passage, usually between two internal organs

fluoroscopy: examination of deep structures by means of roentgen rays

fundoscopy: visual examination of the fundus of the eye

gastrointestinal: relating to the stomach and intestines

genitourinary: relating to the genital areas and urinary tract

geriatrics: the specialty of medicine in which problems of old age are treated

gingivitis: inflammation of the gums of the mouth

glaucoma: a condition in which the lens of the eye is opaque; a disease of the eye in which there is an increase in ocular pressure and hardness of the eye, atrophy of the eye and eventually blindness

glioma: a tumor composed of tissue representing neuralgia

glossitis: inflammation of the tongue

gout: a condition in which the uric acid level is high and there is the sudden onset of arthritis

gravida: number of pregnancies

guaiac: a reagent used in tests for occult blood, especially in the stool

hematemesis: vomiting of blood

hematuria: blood in the urine

hemiplegia: a condition in which one side of the body is paralyzed

hemorrhage: the escape of blood from the blood vessels; bleeding

hepatitis: inflammation of the liver

hepatosplenomegaly: enlargement of the liver and spleen

histologic: the branch of pathology in which the minute structure, composition and function of the tissues are studied

hypertension: abnormally high blood pressure

hypnosis: an artificially induced state of increased amenability to suggestions and commands, provided the suggestions and commands do not conflict with the subject's beliefs or values; an artificially induced state of sleep or semi-consciousness

hypokalemia: an abnormally low amount of potassium in the blood

hyponatremia: an abnormally low amount of sodium in the blood

iatrogenic: a condition, or a problem, resulting from the activity of physicians

idiopathic: something whose cause is unknown

impetigo: an inflammatory skin disease with isolated pustules

inguinal: relating to the groin region

ischemia: deficiency of blood to a part of the body

jaundice: a condition marked by a yellow skin color caused by the depositing of bile pigment in the skin or mucous membranes (also called icterus)

jejunum: the section of small intestine that extends from the duodenum to the ileum

kyphosis: abnormally increased convexity in the curvature of the thoracic spine; a hunchback condition

labium: a fleshy border or edge; a lip

lacrimal: pertaining to tears

laparoscopy: visual exploration of the peritoneal area with a special scope

lateral: pertaining to the side of something

leukocyte: a white blood cell

lipoma: a fatty tumor

lymphadenopathy: disease of the lymph nodes

malaise: a vague feeling of physical discomfort

malleolus: the rounded protrusion on the ankle joint

malleus: the club-shaped or hammer-shaped auditory bone

melena: blackened stools

Meniere's disease: a disease of the auditory system marked by symptoms of deafness, tinnitus, dizziness and pressure in the ears

meninges: the membranes that envelop the brain and spinal cord

menstrual: pertaining to menses, the monthly flow of blood from the uterus

metastasis: the transfer of disease from one organ or part of the body to another organ or part, which is not connected or related to the first organ or part

mnemasthenia: poor memory not attributable to organic disease

musculoskeletal: relating to the muscles and skeleton

myalgia: muscle ache

myoma: a tumor made up of muscular tissue

myopia: the condition of near-sightedness

narcissism: extreme self-love

narcotic: a substance that produces insensibility or stupor; a class of drugs that is regulated by law

neoplasm: an abnormally rapid growth of tissue showing a lack of structural organization

neuralgia: an aching in the nerves

neurologic: relating to the nervous system

neurosis: a functional disorder of the nervous system; an emotional disorder due to unresolved conflicts, with anxiety being its primary characteristic

normocephalic: having a normally shaped head

nystagmus: a rhythmic involuntary movement of the eyes, which movement may be horizontal, vertical, rotary or mixed

ophthalmologic: relating to the study of the eyes

organomegaly: enlargment of the organs, especially the organs of the abdominal region

orthopnea: difficulty breathing in any position other than upright

ossification: the formation or production of bone; the metamorphosis of something into bone

osteomyelitis: inflammation of the bone marrow

osteoporosis: a reduction in the amount of bone; atrophy of the skeleton

otitis: inflammation of the ear

oxytocic: a substance that stimulates uterine movement

para: number of pregnancies ending in births

parenteral: pertaining to the administering of a drug by means other than through the alimentary canal; a drug administered subcutaneously, intramuscularly or intravenously

paresis: a partial or incomplete paralysis

paroxysm: a sudden recurrence or intensification of symptoms; a spasm or seizure

pathology: the study of the nature and cause of disease processes

pediatric: the specialty of medicine in which problems of children are treated

percussion: the act of striking a body part as an aid in making a diagnosis by the sound obtained

phlebitis: inflammation of a blood vein

phlegm: viscous mucus secreted in an abnormally large amount, usually produced by expectoration

pleurisy: a condition of inflammation of the lung membrane

pneumonia: an infection of the lungs, marked by inflammation of the lungs with consolidation

polydipsia: excessive thirst

polyuria: excessive and frequent urination

promontory: a projecting eminence or process

prophylaxis: a substance that prevents an untoward effect or disease

proteinuria: an excessive amount of protein in the urine

pseudomotor: abnormal movements which resemble normal motor movements

psoas: a muscle in the region of the last thoracic and first lumbar vertebrae

pulmonary: pertaining to the lungs

purulent: pertaining to pus; containing or forming pus

psychosis: a mental disorder characterized by deranged personality and loss of contact with reality

pyelography: a radiographic study of the renal pelvis and ureter

radiology: the study of radioactive substances and using radioactive methods to detect and treat disease

reflux: a return flow; regurgitation

rheumatoid: a condition resembling a disorder characterized by inflammation or degeneration of the connective tissues

rhinitis: inflammation of the mucous membrane of the nose

roentgen: the unit of radiation used in diagnostic imaging; an x-ray

Romberg's sign: an inability to maintain balance when the eyes are shut and the feet are in close proximity to each other

rumination: rechewing of food; repetitive meditation

sarcoma: a malignant tumor derived from connective tissue

scaphoid: boat-shaped; a boat-shaped bone in the hand or foot

sclerosis: hardening

serosanguineous: something which contains both blood and serum

sialadenitis: inflammation of the salivary gland

spondylitis: inflammation of the spinal vertebrae

sputum: mucusy matter ejected from the lungs, bronchi and trachea through the mouth

squamous: scaly or platelike

stenosis: narrowing or constriction of a duct or canal

subcutaneous: under the skin

supination: the act of assuming the supine position; turning of the hands or feet inward

syncope: fainting; a temporary state of lack of consciousness due to cerebral ischemia

systolic pressure: the upper reading of the blood pressure; the maximum pressure of the blood that occurs during ventricular contraction

tachycardia: a quickened heart beat rate

tangential: pertaining to suddenly changing to another thought or action; something attached only at one point to the side of another thing

therapeutic: a substance used in therapy or in treating a disease process

thoracic: pertaining to the chest or vertebrae in the thorax area

tic: an involuntary, repetitive twitching of muscles, often in the face or upper trunk

tinnitus: a ringing in the ears

uncinate: hooked or barbed, as in a bone

ventricornu: a horn of gray matter located in the spinal cord

vertigo: an illusion of movement, or the illusion of movement of objects around a person, when movement does not exist; dizziness

xanthoma: a papule, nodule or plaque of yellowish color in the skin, due to lipid deposits

zygoma: the cheek bone

Appendix C

Medical Symbols

Mathematical/Scientific Symbols

Å	angstrom unit	×	multiplied by; times
°	degree	=	equal to
′	foot; minute; univalent	≠	not equal to
″	inch; second; bivalent	≈	approximately equal to
‴	trivalent; 1/12 inch line	>	greater than
μ	micron	≥	greater than or equal to
μμ	micromicron	<	less than
mμ	millimicron or micromilli-meter	≤	less than or equal to
		√	root or square root
π	pi (3.1416... the ratio of circumference to diameter)	$^2\sqrt{}$	square root
		$^3\sqrt{}$	cube root
σ	1/1000 of a second		
μg	microgram	%	percent
:	ratio	#	number; gauge; weight
::	equality between ratios	→	causes the following reaction
∴	therefore	←	is caused by the previous reaction
−	negative (minus)		
+	positive (plus)	Δ	delta; indicates a change
±	plus or minus; positive or negative; not definite (also indicates standard deviation)	↑	increased; elevated
		↓	decreased; depressed
		m-	meta
÷	divided by	o-	ortho

259

p-	para	/	per; of; fraction
°C	degrees centigrade (Celsius)	x^2	chi square (test)
°F	degrees Fahrenheit	Ω	ohm
°K	degrees Kelvin	Σ	sum
∞	infinity		

Prescription Symbols

℞	take	M	mix
p̄	after	O.	pint
ā	before	C	gallon
c̄	with	gr.	grain
s̄	without	tab.	tablet
S.	write	s̄s	one half

Weights and Measures Symbols

$	dollar,	#, lb.	pound (= 16 oz.)
¢	cent,	ft.	foot (= 12 inches)
£	British pound	yd.	yard (= 3 feet)
ƒ	franc	ac.	acre (= 43560 sq. feet)
ʒ , oz.	ounce	mi.	mile (= 5280 feet)
in.	inch	tn.	ton (= 2000 pounds)

Miscellaneous Medical Symbols

*	birth	1°	primary
†	death	2°	secondary
τ	life or lifetime	3°	tertiary
♂	male	?	question or questionable
♀	female		

Appendix D

Reference Values for Common Laboratory Data

D-1   Major Categories of Laboratory Data

Following are the five major categories of laboratory data:

1. hematology
2. urine analysis
3. serology
4. toxicology
5. therapeutic drug monitoring

D-2   Hematology

Following are the normal reference values for laboratory data associated with the blood, also called the complete blood count. (* - asterisk denotes abbreviation is acceptable for use in sections other than laboratory data; all abbreviations are acceptable for use in laboratory data sections.) (Normal values are expressed in conventional units.)

Abbreviation Acceptable *	Reference	Reference Abbrev.	Normal Values
*	alkaline phosphatase	alk. phos.	14–100
	carboxyhemoglobin	carboxy HG	up to 5% of total
	cell counts:		
	-erythrocytes	N/A	4.2–5.9 million/cu mm

Abbreviation Acceptable *	Reference	Reference Abbrev.	Normal Values
	-leukocytes	N/A	4,300–10,800/cu mm
	differential (diff):		
	+myelocytes	myelos	0
*	+band neutrophils	bands	3–5%
*	+segmented neutrophils	segs	54–62%
*	+lymphocytes	lymphs	25–33%
*	+monocytes	monos	3–7%
	+eosinophils	eos	1–3%
	+basophils	basos	0–0.75%
	-platelets	N/A	150,000–350,000 /cu mm
	-reticulocytes	retics	25,000–75,000 /cu mm
	coagulation tests:		
	-bleeding time (Duke)	N/A	1–5 minutes
	-bleeding time (Simplate)	N/A	3–9.5 minutes
	-clot lysis time	N/A	none in 24 hours
	-coagulation time	N/A	5–15 minutes for glass tubes; 19-60 minutes for siliconized tubes
*	-factor VII and other coagulation factors	factor VII	50–150% of normal
*	-fibrin split products	fibrin	negative at 1:4 dilution
	-fibrinogen	N/A	200–400 mg/100 ml
	-fibrinolysis	N/A	0
*	-partial thromboplastin time	PTT	25–38 seconds
*	-prothrombin time	PT	12.0–14.0 seconds

Abbreviation Acceptable *	Reference	Reference Abbrev.	Normal Values
	-tourniquet test	N/A	up to 10 petechiae
	cold hemolysin test	N/A	no hemolysis
*	Coombs test	Coombs	negative
	corpuscular values of erythrocytes:		
*	-mean corpuscular hemoglobin	MCH	27–32 pico-grams/RBC
*	-mean corpuscular volume	MCV	86–98 cu μm
*	-mean corpuscular hemoglobin concentration	MCHC	32–36%
	haptoglobin	N/A	40–336 mg/100 ml
	hematocrit	H, Hct or crit	37–52%
	hemoglobin	H or Hg	1218 grams/100 ml
	hemoglobin A_{1C}	A1C or H_{A1C}	3–5% of total
	hemoglobin A_2	A2 or H_{A2}	1.5–3% of total
	hemoglobin, plasma	plasma Hg	up to 5 mg/100 ml
	methemoglobin	m-Hg	1–130 mg/100 ml
*	sedimentation rate	sed rate	1–20 mm per hour
	bone marrow differential:		
	-myeloblasts	myelos	0.3–5.0%
	-promyelocytes	promyelos	1–8%
	-neutrophilic myelocytes	neutro-myelos	5–19%
	-eosinophilic myelocytes	eo myelos	0.5–3.0%
	-basophilic myelocytes	baso myelos	0.0–0.5%
*	-polymorphonuclear neutrophils	polys or polymorphs	7–30%
	-polymorphonuclear eosinophils	poly eos	0.5–4.0%

Abbreviation Acceptable *	Reference	Reference Abbrev.	Normal Values
	-polymorphonuclear basophils	poly basophils	0.0–0.7%
*	-lymphocytes	lymphs	3–17%
	-plasma cells	N/A	0–2%
*	-monocytes	monos	0.5–5.0%
	-reticulum cells	retics	0.1–2.0%
	-megakaryocytes	N/A	0.3–3.0%
	-pronormoblasts	N/A	1–8%
	-normoblasts	N/A	7–32%

D-3   Urine Analysis

Following are the normal reference values for laboratory data associated with the urine:

Abbreviation Acceptable *	Reference	Reference Abbrev.	Normal Values
	acetone and acetoacetate	N/A	0 or negative
	Addis count:		
	-erythrocytes	N/A	up to 130,000/24 hours
	-leukocytes	N/A	up to 650,000/24 hours
*	-casts	N/A	up to 2,000/24 hours
	albumin	N/A	negative
	aldosterone	N/A	3–20 µg/24 hours
	alpha-amino nitrogen	N/A	50–200 mg/24 hours
	ammonia nitrogen	N/A	20–70 mEq/24 hours
	amylase	N/A	24–76 units/ml

Abbreviation Acceptable *	Reference	Reference Abbrev.	Normal Values
	bilirubin	bili	negative
	calcium	Ca	less than 300 mg/day
	catecholamines:		
	-epinephrine	epi	under 20 µg/day
	-norepinephrine	norepi	under 100 µg/day
*	chloride	Cl	110–250 mEq/24 hours
	chorionic gonadotropin, human	HCG	0 (elevation denotes pregnancy)
*	copper	Cu	up to 50 µg/24 hours
*	creatine	N/A	under 100 mg/day or less than 6% of creatinine (higher during pregnancy and in
	creatinine	creat	15–25 mg/kg of body weight per day
	creatinine clearance	N/A	105–150 ml per minute
	cystine/cysteine	N/A	0 or negative
	glucose	sugar	less than 250 mg/24 hours
	hemoglobin and myoglobin	N/A	negative
	5-hydroxyindoleacetic acid	N/A	1–26 mg/day (women lower than men)
	17-hydroxysteroids	N/A	3–8 mg/day (women lower than men)
	17-ketosteroids	N/A	4–18 mg/24 hours

Abbreviation Acceptable *	Reference	Reference Abbrev.	Normal Values
*	magnesium	Mg	6.0–8.5 mEq/24 hours
*	lead	Pb	0.08 µg/ml, or 120 µg/day or less
	osmolality	Osm	38–1,400 mOsm/kg of water
	potential of hydrogen concentration (hydrogen ion concentration)	pH	4.6–8.0, average 6.0
*	phenolsulfonphthalein excretion	PSP	25% or more in 15 min., 40% or more in 30 min., 55% or more in 2 hours
*	phenylpyruvic acid	PPA	negative
	phosphorus	phos	0.9–1.3 g/24 hours
	porphobilinogen	PBG	0 or negative
	porphyrins:		
	-coproporphyrin	N/A	50–250 µg/24 hours
	-uroporphyrin	N/A	10-30 µg/24 hours
*	potassium	K	25–100 mEq/24 hours
	pregnanediol	N/A	0.2–1.4 mg/24 hours (increases markedly during luteal phase of menstruation)
	pregnanetriol	N/A	less than 2.5 mg/24 hours in adults
	protein	N/A	qualitatively negative; quantitatively 10–150 /24 hours
*	sodium	Na	130-260 mEq /24 hours

Abbreviation Acceptable *	Reference	Reference Abbrev.	Normal Values
	specific gravity	spec. grav.	1.003–1.030
	titratable acidity	N/A	20–40 mEq/24 hours
	urate	N/A	200–500 mg/24 hours (normal diet)
	urobilinogen	N/A	up to 1.0 Ehrlich units/2 hours
	uroporphyrin	N/A	0–30 µg/day
*	vanillylmandelic acid	VMA	up to 9 mg/24 hours

D-4   Serology

Following are the normal reference values for laboratory data associated with blood, plasma and serum.

{ ♣ denotes common SMAC (superior mesenteric artery count) value}

{ ♥ denotes common ABG (arterial blood gas) value}

{ ♠ denotes liver panel value}

Abbreviation Acceptable *	Reference	Reference Abbrev.	Normal Values
	acetoacetate and acetone	N/A	negative
*	adrenocorticotropic hormone, serum	ACTH	10–80 pico-grams/milliliter
♠ ♣	albumin	N/A	3.5–5.0 g/100 ml
	aldolase, serum	N/A	1.3–8.2 units/liter
♠ ♣	alkaline phosphatase	alk. phos.	14-100
	ammonia, plasma	N/A	12–55 µmol/liter
	amylase, serum	N/A	4–25 units/ml
	anion gap	N/A	8–16 mEq/l
*	antinuclear antibodies	ANA	no change
	ascorbic acid, blood	N/A	0.4–1.5 mg/100 ml

Abbreviation Acceptable *	Reference	Reference Abbrev.	Normal Values
	base excess, blood	N/A	0 2 mEq/l
	bicarbonate	bicarb	23–29 mEq/l
	bile acids, serum	N/A	0.3–3.0 mg/dl
♠ ♣	bilirubin, serum, total	bili.	up to 1.0 mg/100 ml
♠ ♣	bilirubin, serum, direct	bili.	up to 0.4 mg/100 ml
	bromsulphalein	BSP	less than 5%
♣	calcium, serum	Ca	8.5–10.5 mg/100 mg
* ♣ ♥	carbon dioxide content, serum	CO_2	24–30 mEq/l
* ♥	carbon dioxide tension	PCO_2	35–45 mm Hg
	carotene, serum	N/A	50–300 µg/100 ml
	ceruloplasmin, serum	N/A	27–37 mg/100 ml
♣ ♥	chloride, serum	Cl	100-106 mEq/l
♠ ♣	cholesterol, serum	N/A	150-250 mg/100 ml
	cholinesterase	N/A	0.5–1.3 pH units
	copper, serum	Cu	100–200 µg/100 ml
	cortisol, plasma	N/A	6–23 µg/100 ml
	creatine, serum	N/A	0.2–0.8 mg/100 ml
*	creatine phosphokinase	CPK	up to 78 units/milliliter (two-fold in females)
♣	creatinine, serum	creat	0.6-1.5 mg/100 ml
	fatty acids, serum	FA	190–420 mg/100 ml
	ferritin, serum	N/A	20–200 ng/ml
	fibrinogen, serum	N/A	200-400 mg/100 ml
	folate, serum	N/A	5–21 ng/ml

Abbreviation Acceptable *	Reference	Reference Abbrev.	Normal Values
*	follicle stimulating hormone	FSH	4–30 milliunits/milliliter
* ♠	gamma glutamyltransferase	GGT	4–32 milliunits/milliliter
	gastrin, serum	N/A	0–200 pico-grams/milliliter
	glucose (fasting):		
♣	-blood	N/A	60–100 mg/100 ml
♣	-plasma or serum	N/A	70–115 mg/100 ml
	growth hormone, serum	N/A	100–200 mg/100 ml
	immunoglobulins, serum:		
*	-IgG	N/A	550–1900 mg/100 ml
*	-IgA	N/A	60–333 mg/100 ml
*	-IgM	N/A	45–145 mg/100 ml
	insulin, plasma	N/A	5–25 microunits /milliliter
	iodine, serum	I	3.5–8.0 μg/100 ml
	iron, serum	Fe	75–175 μg/100 ml
	iron binding capacity:		
	-total	N/A	250–410 μg/100 ml
	-saturation	N/A	20–55%
	lactate, blood	N/A	0.6–1.8 mEq/l
* ♣	lactate dehydrogenase, serum	LDH	45–90 units/liter
	lipase, serum	N/A	up to 2 units/ml
	lipids, total, serum	N/A	450–850 mg/100 ml
*	lipoproteins, high density	HDL	39–90 mg/dl
*	lipoproteins, low density	LDL	57.37–171.00 mg/dl

Abbreviation Acceptable *	Reference	Reference Abbrev.	Normal Values
*	luteinizing hormone, serum	LH	5–22 milliunits/milliliter
	magnesium, serum	Mg	1.5–2.0 mEq/l
	nitrogen, nonprotein serum	N	15–35 mg/100 ml
	osmolality, serum	Osm	285–295 m Osm/kg
	oxygen, blood:		
* ♥	-capacity	O$_2$	16–24 volumes percent
* ♥	-content (arterial)	O$_2$	15–23 volumes percent
* ♥	-saturation (arterial)	O$_2$	94–100% of capacity
* ♥	-tension	pO$_2$	75–100 mm Hg
	phosphatase, serum:		
	-acid	N/A	0.01–0.63 sigma units/milliliter
	-alkaline	N/A	13–39 units/liter (higher in infants andadolescents)
♣	phosphorus	N/A	3.0–4.5 mg/100 ml
♣♥	potassium, serum	K	3.5–5.0 mEq/l
♥	potential of hydrogen, arterial, blood	pH	7.35–7.45
♣	protein, serum, total	N/A	6–8 g/100 ml
	protein electrophoresis:		
	-albumin	N/A	3.5–5.5 g/100 ml
	-albumin	N/A	3.5–5.5 g/100 ml
	-globulin	N/A	0.2–1.7 grams/100 ml
	pyruvate, blood	N/A	0.01–0.11 mEq/l

Abbreviation Acceptable *	Reference	Reference Abbrev.	Normal Values
♣ ♥	sodium, serum	Na	136–145 mEq/l
	sulfates, inorganic, serum	SO₄	0.8–1.2mg/100 ml
	syphilis serology:		
*	-rapid plasma reagin	RPR	negative
*	-Venereal Disease Research Laboratory	VDRL	negative
	testosterone, plasma:		
	-males	N/A	275–875 ng/100 ml
	-females	N/A	23–75 ng/100 ml
	-pregnant	N/A	38–190 ng/100 ml
*	thyroid stimulating hormone	TSH	0–7 microunits/ml
*	thyroxine, serum	T₄	1.0–9.9 µg/100ml
*	thyroxine binding globulin	TBG	10–26 µg/100 ml
	transaminase, serum:		
* ♣	-aspartate aminotransferase	SGOT	0–19 milliunits/milliliter
* ♣	-alanine aminotransferase	SGPT	0–17 milliunits/milliliter
♣	triglycerides, serum	TG	30–190 mg/100 ml
*	tri-iodothyronine, uptake	T₃	25–38%
	urate, serum	N/A	1.5–8.0 mg/100 ml
*	urea nitrogen, blood	BUN	10–20 mg/100 ml
♣	urea nitrogen, serum	SUN	11–23 mg/100 ml
♣	uric acid	N/A	0.5–1 g/day
	vitamin A, serum	N/A	20–80 µg/100 ml
	vitamin B₁₂, serum	N/A	180–900 pico grams/milliliter

D-5   Toxicology

Following are the toxic levels for common toxic substances:

Abbreviation Acceptable *	Reference	Reference Abbrev.	Toxic Levels
	arsenic, blood	As	3.5–7.2 µg/100 ml
	arsenic, urine	As	< 100 µg/24 hours
*	bromides, serum	Br	>17 mEq/l
*	carbon monoxide, blood	CO	up to 5% saturation (symptoms occur with 20% saturation)
*	ethanol, blood	ETOH	less than 0.005%
	-marked intoxication	"	0.3–0.4%
	-alcoholic stupor	"	0.4–0.5%
	-coma	"	0.5%
*	lead, blood	Pb	0–40 µg/100ml
	lead, urine	Pb	<100 µg/24 hours
*	mercury, urine	Hg	< µg/24 hours

D-6   Therapeutic Drug Monitoring

Following are the therapeutic ranges and toxic levels for common medications used in pharmacotherapy:

Drug Name	Therapeutic Range	Toxic Levels
antibiotics:		
-amikacin	15–25 µg/ml	>35 µg/ml
-chloramphenicol	10–20 µg/ml	>25 µg/ml
-gentamicin	5–10 µg/ml	>12 µg/ml
-tobramycin	5–10 µg/ml	>12 µg/ml
anticonvulsants:		

Drug Name	Therapeutic Range	Toxic Levels
-carbamazepine	5–12 µg/ml	>15 µg/ml
-ethosuximide	40–80 µg/ml	>150 µg/ml
-phenobarbital	10–25 µg/ml	varies
-phenytoin	10–20 µg/ml	>20 µg/ml
-primidone	4–12 µg/ml	>15 µg/ml
-valproic acid	50–100 µg/ml	>200 µg/ml
anti-inflammatory agents:		
-acetaminophen	10–20 µg/ml	>250 µg/ml
-salicylate	100–250 µg/ml	>300 µg/ml
bronchodilators:		
-theophylline	10–20 µg/ml	>20 µg/ml
cardiovascular drugs:		
-digitoxin	15–25 ng/m	>25 ng/ml
-digoxin	0.8–2 ng/ml	>2.4 ng/ml
-disopyramide	2–4 µg/ml	>7 µg/ml
-lidocaine	1.5–5 µg/ml	>7 ng/ml
-procainamide	4–10 µg/ml	>16 µg/ml
-propranolol	50–100 ng/ml	varies
-quinidine	2–5 µg/ml	>10 µg/ml
psychopharmacologic drugs:	120–150 ng/ml	>500 ng/ml
-chlordiazepoxide	1–3 µg/ml	>5 mg/ml
-desipramine	150–250 ng/ml	>500 ng/ml
-diazepam	0.5–2.5 µg/ml	>5 µg/ml
-imipramine	150–250 ng/ml	>500 ng/ml
-lithium	0.8–1.5 mEq/l	>2.0 mEq/l
-nortriptyline	50–150 ng/ml	>500 ng/ml

D-7   **Additional Laboratory Data**

In addition to the above values, other laboratory testing of systemic fluids and functioning is often done. These include reference values for: cerebrospinal fluid, gastric analysis, gastrointestinal absorption tests, feces analysis, semen analysis, pancreatic function tests, liver function tests, kidney function tests, thyroid function tests, endocrine function tests, and immunologic procedures.

D-8   **Other Laboratory Notes**

Keep the following points in mind when transcribing laboratory data:

a.   Never begin a sentence with an abbreviation, even in laboratory data.

b.   Always use lowercase "p" and uppercase "H" for pH.

c.   SMAC values can also be abbreviated SMA or Chem (for Chemistry). SMAC values can be tested either with 4 values (the electrolytes - sodium, potassium, carbon dioxide and chloride), 6 or 7 values (SMAC-6 or SMAC-7, or Chem-6 or Chem-7) or 9, 11, 15, 19 and 22 values.

d.   Always use a "0" to hold the place before a decimal (e.g., 0.5, not .5).

e.   Note that many values increase from three- to ten-fold during pregnancy.

Bibliography

Accreditation Manual for Hospitals. Chicago: Joint Commission on Accreditation of Hospitals, 1984.

Atkinson, Phillips S. and Deborah Begg. *Medical Office Practice.* 4th ed. Cincinnati: South-Western Publishing Co., 1990.

Billups, Norman F., and Shirley M. Billups. *American Drug Index.* 36th ed. Philadelphia: J. B. Lippincott Co., 1992.

Chabner, Davi-Ellen. *The Language of Medicine.* 2nd ed. Philadelphia: W. B. Saunders Co., 1981.

Conerly, Donna L. and Wanda Lott. *Forrest General Medical Center.* Cincinnati: South-Western Publishing Co., 1986.

Davis, Neil M. *Medical Abbreviations: 5500 Conveniences at the Expense of Communications and Safety.* 4th ed. Huntingdon Valley, PA: Neil M. Davis Assoc., 1988.

DeGowin, Richard L. *DeGowin & DeGowin's Bedside Diagnostic Examination.* 5th ed. New York: Macmillan Publishing Company, 1987.

Dirckx, John H. *H & P: A Nonphysician's Guide.* 2nd rev. ed. Modesto, Calif.: PrimaVera Publications, 1991.

Dorland's Illustrated Medical Dictionary. 27th ed. W. B. Saunders Co., 1987.

Fowler, H. Ramsey and Jane E. Aaron. *The Little, Brown Handbook.* 4th ed. Glenview, Illinois: Scott, Foresman and Company, 1989.

Gense, Carol. *Medical and Dental Associates, P.C.: Insurance Forms Preparation.* Cincinnati: South-Western Publishing Co., 1990.

House, Clifford R. and Kathie Sigler. *Reference Manual.* 7th ed. Cincinnati: South-Western Publishing Co., 1989.

Humphrey, Doris. *Contemporary Medical Office Procedures.* Cincinnati: South-Western Publishing Co., 1990.

Humphrey, Doris and Kathie Sigler. *The Modern Medical Office: A Reference Manual.* Cincinnati: South-Western Publishing Co., 1990.

Lewis, Norman, ed. *The New Roget's Thesaurus of the English Language in Dictionary Form.* 23rd impression. New York: G. P. Putnam's Sons, 1978.

Lorenzini, Jean A. *Medical Phrase Index.* Oradell, N.J.: Medical Economics Book Co., 1978.

Medical Abbreviations Handbook. 2nd ed. Oradell, N.J.: Medical Economics Book Co., 1983.

The Merck Manual. 14th ed. Rahway, N.J.: Merck Sharp & Dohme Research Laboratories, 1982.

Miller, Alan R. *The ABC's of MS-DOS.* 2nd ed. Alameda, Calif.: Sybex, Inc., 1988.

Miller, Benjamin F., and Claire Brackman Keane. *Encyclopedia and Dictionary of Medicine, Nursing and Allied Health.* 3rd ed. Philadelphia: W. B. Saunders Co., 1983.

MS-DOS Version 3, Basic Concepts and Features. Vol. 1. St. Joseph, Mich.: Zenith Data Systems Corporation, 1986.

Novak, Mary Ann, Patricia Ireland and Frederick J. Frensilli. *Hillcrest Medical Center: Beginning Medical Transcription Course.* Cincinnati: South-Western Publishing Co., 1990.

Parham, Christine A. *Psychology: Studying the Behavior of People.* 2nd ed. Cincinnati: South-Western Publishing Co., 1988.

Physicians' Desk Reference. 46th ed. Oradell, N.J.: Medical Economics Book Co., 1992.

Pyle, Vera. *Current Medical Terminology.* 3rd ed. Modesto, Calif.: Prima Vera Publications, 1990.

Roe-Hafer, Ann. *The Medical & Health Sciences Word Book.* 2nd ed. Boston: Houghton Mifflin Co., 1982.

Sloane, Sheila B. *The Medical Word Book.* 2nd ed. Philadelphia: W. B. Saunders Co., 1982.

Sloane, Sheila B., and John L. Dussau. *A Word Book in Pathology and Laboratory Medicine.* Philadelphia: W. B. Saunders Co., 1984.

Sormunen, Carolee. *Terminology for Allied Health Professionals.* 2nd ed. Cincinnati: South-Western Publishing Co., 1990.

Stedman's Medical Dictionary. 24th ed. Baltimore: The Williams & Wilkins Co., 1982.

Style Guide for Medical Transcription. Modesto, Calif.: American Association of Medical Transcription, 1985.

Taylor, Dorothy A. and B. Lewis Keeling. *Medical Pegboard Procedures.* Cincinnati: South-Western Publishing Co., 1987.

Tessier, Claudia. *The Surgical Word Book.* Philadelphia: W. B. Saunders Co., 1981.

Thomas, Clayton L., ed. *Taber's Cyclopedic Medical Dictionary.* 16th ed. Philadelphia: F.A. Davis Co., 1989.

Using WordPerfect 5.1, Special Edition. Carmel, Illinois: Que Corporation, 1989.

Webster's Ninth New Collegiate Dictionary. Springfield, Mass.: Merriam-Webster, Inc., 1983.

Webster's Third New International Dictionary of the English Language, Unabridged. Springfield, Mass.: Merriam-Webster, Inc., 1983.

WordPerfect for IBM Personal Computers. Version 5.0. Orem, Utah: WordPerfect Corporation, 1989.

Zedlitz, Robert. *Getting a Job in Health Care*. Cincinnati: South-Western Publishing Co., 1987.

Index

A

Abbreviations, 107–119
  and capitalization, 127
  general rules for, 107–108
  lowercase, 114–115
  metric, 117–118
  mixed case, 115–117
  uppercase, 108–114
Acronyms,70–71
Adjectives, 81
Adverbs, 81–82
Ages, patient, and figures, 137
All-, hyphenation of, 101
Allergies, and capitaalization,126
Antonyms, 72
Apgar ratings, 140
Apostrophes, 94,
  in contractions, 104–105
Arabic numerals, 140
Articles, 82–83

B

Blood pressure, and figures, 139
Brackets, 97
Brand names, capitalization of 127
Brief forms, 105–106
Bytes, Computer, 16

C

Cancer stages and grades, 140
Capitalization, 120–128
  in headings, 120–123
Cardiac murmur grades, and Roman numerals, 140
Central Processing Unit (CPU), 14, 238
Chart notes

formats for, 42
  types of, 41
Check-up, 41
  v. check up, 101–102
Chemical symbols, 116, 139
Clauses, 82
Colons, 92–93
Commas, 89–92
Commonly confused/misspelled words, 144–150
Compound adjectives, 100
Compound words, 101
  and hyphenation, 99–100, 102
Conjunctions, 83
Consultation Report, 27, 34 (sample of)
Contractions, 104–105
Correspondence, medical office
  formats for, 42
  types of, 41
CPU. *See* Central Processing Unit
Cranial nerves, 140
Cursor, 13

D

Dashes, 95–96
Dates, 118, 142
Decimals, 138
Degrees, educational, 119
Departments
  hospital, 128
  and medical, 128
Dictation, 7–10
Directories, in DOS, 238–243
Discharge Summary, 28, 38–39 (sample of)
Diseases, and capitalization 124
Disk drive, 17

279

U, V, W